27

-5. JA

27

2

M

C

The Great Sarah
The Life of Mrs Siddons

By the same author

The Starke Sisters
Charlotte
Kelford Dig

Nigel Rides Away
The Cave in the Cliff
The Pageant

Sarah Siddons by Gainsborough

The Great Sarah

The Life of Mrs Siddons

Kathleen Mackenzie

Evans Brothers Limited London

Published by Evans Brothers Limited,
Montague House, Russell Square,
London, W.C.1.

Set in 11 on 12 point Intertype Baskerville and printed in Great
Britain by Cox and Wyman Ltd., Fakenham
237 35035 1/8001   PR 4573

Contents

Illustrations

Sarah Siddons by Gainsborough   Frontispiece
Mr and Mrs Roger Kemble; John Kemble
Sarah Siddons in some of her most famous parts
The interior of Drury Lane Theatre:
a Bill announcing Sarah's appearance in *Richard III*
                                    between pages 64 and 65

A sketch of Sarah by Thomas Lawrence; Sir Thomas Lawrence
The poster announcing new prices at Covent Garden Theatre
The interiors of the old and new Covent Garden Theatres
Cecilia, Sally and George Siddons; Charles Kemble
                                    between pages 112 and 113

For permission to reproduce photographs in this book, the author and publishers are indebted to Harry R. Beard Theatre Collection; Mary Evans Picture Library; Raymond Mander and Joe Mitchenson Theatre Collection; the Trustees of the National Gallery; Radio Times Hulton Picture Library.

1 The Curtain Rises

One evening, in the year 1767, an audience of Worcester townsfolk gathered in the King's Head Inn to see a performance of the play *Charles the First*. Candles, stuck into bottles and smoking and guttering in the draughts, stood in a row before the dusty, makeshift curtains and behind those curtains Mr Roger Kemble's Company of Comedians were ready to perform the play. There were several of his own children in his Company and among them was a thin, dark, eleven-year-old girl, with enormous eyes and very expressive eyebrows. Her name was Sarah, and she was to become the greatest tragic actress of the English stage.

Ever since she was born in the little old inn called The Shoulder of Mutton at Brecon in Wales, on 5 July 1755, Sarah, and the brothers and sisters born after her, had travelled round with her parents from town to town in the West Country, where Roger Kemble's Company acted their plays in public-house rooms, barns and inn courtyards. There were few proper theatres so they had to make do with what accommodation they could get.

The first time Sarah ever appeared on the stage was when she was between three and four years old. It was an unnerving experience for her because the moment she got down near the footlights she was greeted with a roar of disapproval. Audiences in the eighteenth century were extremely outspoken and because they thought she was too young to be allowed to perform they said so. Poor Sarah, of course, imagined they were angry with her and backed away upstage to where her mother was watching her in the wings. Either Mrs Kemble thought it would be bad for Sarah to start her stage career in this way, or she was determined not to be browbeaten by an audience, because she took her daughter by the hand and led her down to the footlights again. Mrs Kemble was tall, handsome and authoritative, and her presence alone quietened the audience, so that Sarah was able to drop her mother's hand and standing alone, recite her poem. It was called *The Fable of the Boys and the Frogs* and began :

> ' 'Tis death to us, though sport to you
> Unthinking, cruel boys . . .'

The audience was quiet while she was speaking and when she had finished, because they admired her pluck and thought she recited well she got thunderous applause. Sarah was nervous before she went on the stage all her life, but with such an alarming first experience it is not strange that she was.

The young Kembles led an unusual life for children, trundling from town to town in a shabby old coach, the scenery and properties for the plays following in wagons. When they arrived in a town the family would put up at an inn and then Mr Kemble would find some place in which they could perform their plays. There was still a strong Puritanical spirit abroad in England at that time – the Puritans thought plays the work of the Devil and theatrical companies were often refused a licence to act. No difference was made by those who disapproved between respectable travelling companies like Roger Kemble's and the riotous, drunken strolling players who were also on the road. One Mayor of Worcester even threatened to imprison any players who came to the town, and attacked them with sticks and stones. Because concerts were allowed, companies got over the lack of a play licence by giving a concert and sandwiching the play in between musical items. Sometimes it was not even safe to make a charge for the play, and Mr Kemble on occasion got round this by selling tooth-powder at two shillings, one shilling, or sixpence at a friendly shop near by and giving the purchasers free admission to the theatre.

Actors stayed in a town just as long as they could get an audience; then they moved on. They used to advertise themselves by processing through the town. First would come a child on whose head was balanced a drum which one of the actors would beat, and then there would be a procession of the other players in costume. Sarah was sometimes the child who carried the drum, and the beautiful carriage of her head may have come from having to balance it. Sometimes she was promoted to walking in the procession. When she became famous a man remembered seeing her parading through a town – a little girl in white satin and spangles, her train held up by her brother John, dressed in black velvet.

Theatrical companies had other ways of advertising too; they printed handbills and tacked them up on walls and doors, or distributed them to anyone who would take one. A number were handed out on 12 February 1767, one of which has survived. It reads:

MR KEMBLE'S COMPANY OF COMEDIANS
At the Theatre of the King's Head this evening will be performed
A Concert of Music
(To begin exactly at Six o'clock). Tickets to be had at the usual places.
Between the parts of the Concert will be presented *gratis* a celebrated historical play (*never performed here*) called
CHARLES THE FIRST
The Characters to be presented in ancient habits *according to the fashion of those times.*

There were a number of the Kemble family in the cast:

General Fairfax	Mr Roger Kemble
Lady Fairfax	Mrs Kemble
James, Duke of York	Master J. Kemble
Duke of Gloucester	Miss F. Kemble
Princess Elizabeth	Miss Kemble

Also among the players was Mr William Siddons, as the Duke of Richmond. He had only recently joined Mr Kemble's Company. He was tall, fair, handsome and a rather solemn young man, who played the juvenile leads. Mr and Mrs Kemble were pleased with him because, though he was no genius, he could play both tragedy and comedy, was very personable and could learn his lines more quickly than anyone they had ever had before. It was true he forgot them as quickly when the need to remember them had passed, but then it did not matter; what mattered when actors were appearing in a different play almost every night was that they should be able to memorize their parts very quickly.

William's father kept The London Apprentice, a public house in Walsall and he wanted his son to be a barber. But William, after he had done some acting with friends in Walsall found he so much preferred the stage that he determined to make it his career, and after playing with various companies for a year he joined Mr Kemble's.

The Kemble children were nearly all tall for their ages, many of them dark and all good looking. Their father gave them parts whenever he could. In 1767 there were six of them: Sarah, who was eleven and a half; John just ten; Stephen, nearly nine; Frances, just seven; Elizabeth nearly six; and Anne, the baby, who was not yet three. There had been another little girl who had died. They had all grown up in and about the theatre. Stephen, in fact, had very nearly been born on the stage – Mrs Kemble had only just had time to finish a performance (she was playing Anne Boleyn) before he arrived.

Mr Kemble was a Roman Catholic, his wife was an Anglican, and they had decided that the boys should be brought up in their father's faith and the girls in their mother's. Mrs Kemble probably took more trouble with her side of the family than Mr Kemble did with his, because Sarah grew up with an uncomplicated, unshakeable faith which she kept all her life. She was always a great believer in prayer, even as a little girl. When she was about eight she was invited to a very special garden party, and for it her mother gave her a pink dress which was most becoming to her dark good looks and was possibly the nicest frock she had ever had. But it was not a dress for wet weather and she was afraid anyway that if it rained the party would be put off. She desperately wanted fine weather, but on the night before the party the weather looked very doubtful. Sarah, matter-of-factly, but with great confidence, decided she must do her part in dealing with the situation by asking God to help. She looked out the prayer for fine weather in her prayer book, and went to bed holding the book firmly clasped to her, opened at this prayer. She woke very early in the morning and was dismayed to hear pelting rain – rain that would certainly put an end to any party. She was sick with disappointment and was about to put her prayer book away, her faith in prayer somewhat shaken, when she saw it was the prayer for *rain* she had been holding so tightly against her. Obviously it was impossible to be surprised that God should have sent rain if that was what one had asked for, so she hurriedly turned to the prayer for fine weather and made quite sure this time which prayer she held to her. When she woke again, at getting-up time, the sun was shining brilliantly. It seemed to her a very good proof of how helpful prayer was, and she never forgot the episode.

Mrs Kemble was a strict mother, but her children were fond of her and admired her, and they all loved the life they led. Their parents, however, did not think that just acting in plays or seeing them rehearsed gave them enough education, so whenever they stayed for any time in one town they sent their children, or the elder ones, to school. Mr and Mrs Kemble were anxious too that Sarah should cultivate her music, so she had lessons in singing and in playing the harpsichord. She had a true, sweet, though not very powerful singing voice and though still so young she sang in the concerts and even, because she was tall, played the heroine in the operas which were part of the Kembles' repertoire.

When *Charles the First* was well received and it seemed reasonably certain that financially it would be worth staying in Worcester for some time, Sarah and John were sent to school there. Mrs Kemble was the person who dealt with this; it was always she who made the arrangements and decisions. Her husband left nearly everything to her. He knew that but for his wife his Company would not have been as successful as it was – he was too easy going. It was his wife who kept discipline among the family and the players. She pampered no one and expected, and got, hard work. Because of this the Kembles' Company was not only respectable, but had far higher standards of acting than was usual among strolling players.

Mrs Kemble spoke beautifully. She had a particularly clear voice and without any effort or exaggeration could always be heard clearly. Sarah inherited this voice and in her case it was not only beautiful, but flexible and expressive – she could make it indicate every gradation of mood. As expressive as her voice were her eyes. They were enormous and beautifully shaped, dark and with long, curling lashes, and with her mobile eyebrows she could use them to make people understand exactly what she was feeling, so that even when she was not speaking audiences were to find themselves watching her rather than other players.

Mrs Kemble sent Sarah to Thornlea House School, whose headmistress was a Miss Harris. Sarah was not happy there at first. Miss Harris was just and not unkind, but she was stern and the girls were not easy to get on with. Because Sarah's parents were travelling actors they behaved as if she were inferior. They did not exactly snub her – it was almost impossible to do so because, with her, shyness took the form of being dignified and quiet – but they were standoffish. Sarah did not push herself forward, but she did not let herself be trampled on either – if they were not friendly she would go her way and let other people go theirs. Gradually, however, the girls' opinion changed. First of all Sarah's knowledge of Shakespeare and Milton impressed them (she had always adored Milton; from a little girl she had read and re-read him and he remained her favourite poet all her life) and when a school play was suggested the barriers began to go down. The most superior girls found that they had been mistaken in Sarah Kemble – she was a simple, friendly person who not only enjoyed helping, but was able to do so. She acted far better than any other girl in the school, and had far better ideas about where people should stand in a scene and what they should do. For making costumes she was invaluable. No one but Sarah would have thought of using sugar paper to make a sackback – a complicated part of a fashionable dress that hung from the neck to the floor and was attached to the dress between the wide hoops of the skirt.

Although they were anxious to educate their children, if they were needed on the stage Mr and Mrs Kemble let them miss school in order to act. Sarah appeared on three occasions that year at Worcester. She was Edward v, the boy king in Shakespeare's *Richard III* (John played Edward's younger brother, Richard, Duke of York) and in an opera, *Love in a Village* she played Rosetta, the heroine. William Siddons was the hero and Fanny Kemble, who was only seven, played a housemaid – a very diminutive one even if, like the rest of her family, she was tall for her age.

Sarah's third appearance was in another play of Shakespeare's. It was announced on 16 April that 'Mr Kemble's Company of Comedians would appear in a celebrated comedy, called *The Tempest, or the Enchanted Island*, with all the scenery, machinery, music, monsters, and the decorations proper to be given, entirely new. The performance will open with a representation of a tempestuous sea (in perpetual agitatior   ) storm, in which the usurper's ship is wrecked; the wreck ends ʍɪʌn a beautiful shower of fire; and the whole to conclude with a calm sea, on which appears Neptune, poetick god of the ocean, and his royal consort, Amphitrite, in a chariot, drawn by sea-horses, etc., etc.'

The audience on that night would not have seen Shakespeare's play of *The Tempest* as we know it, but a version added to and altered by Dryden. In the eighteenth century it was not considered deplorable to alter famous plays, it was done all the time. Plots were changed, characters omitted or added, and spectacular shows, such as the appearance of Neptune, and Amphitrite with their seahorses considered admirable additions, however little bearing they had on the play.

How the Kembles managed the tempestuous sea and the sea-horses we do not know, but we know that Sarah made an enchanting Ariel. Someone who saw it afterwards described her performance, and said : 'She darted hither and thither with such airy grace; there was something so sprite-like in her free swiftness of motion; she seemed to be so entirely a creature born of the loves of a breeze and a sunbeam, that the whole audience broke into frantic applause at the end of the play.'

It was moments like these that made acting so thrilling to Sarah. It never crossed her mind that she could be anything but an actress, and like all actresses she meant, one day, to be famous.

2 Early Scenes

In the autumn of 1767 the Kembles moved on from Worcester.
While they were there Mrs Kemble had another baby who died – a
little girl they called Lucy, and on November 3rd there was another
break in the family; John went to Sedgerly Park School. He took
with him 4 suits, 12 shirts, 12 pairs of stockings, 6 pairs of shoes,
4 hats, 2 Daily Companions (religious books), a Half Manual, knives,
forks, spoons, *Aesop's Fables*, combs, brush, 8 handkerchiefs and
8 nightcaps. It seems a fairly lavish outfit (except for the number
of handkerchiefs), but much of it was to last him for the four years
he was to stay at school. As he went as a boarder he was not able
to act for his father, but Sarah left Thornlea House when her parents
left Worcester. They could not spare her and now that she was
getting tall enough to play a young heroine convincingly there were
more and more parts for her.

Travelling in those days was not quick; certainly not for family
travel. Vehicles were large and heavy and a day's journey would
probably be only about twenty miles and this would involve stopping
once or twice and changing horses. The Kembles had an old lumber-
ing coach into which the whole family was squashed and which was
drawn, almost at walking pace, from town to town, followed by two
great wagons piled with scenery, properties and wicker hampers of
costumes. The rest of the Company went by stage-coach, sweltering
with heat and covered with dust in summer, and frozen in the
winter. It was an endlessly roving life – the Kembles never had a
fixed home. And it was a life of constant change and equally constant
similarity because, however often they moved, they were always
getting ready for the same plays and playing in the same unwarmed

rooms or barns or shabby theatres. Everyone in the Company had to be ready to do anything at a moment's notice; Sarah's jobs varied from playing the heroine in an opera, taking the lead or a tiny part in a play, helping with the costumes, or even, as she was once seen, standing in the wings all alone, knocking a pair of snuffers against a candlestick to make the sound of a windmill's sails clacking round.

The Kembles acted all the favourite plays of the day, and Sarah took more and more of the leading parts. Once, when they were at Stourbridge some young officers decided to put on *The Grecian Daughter* (a very favourite play at the time) in a barn at the back of the Old Bell Inn, and they asked if Sarah could be the heroine, Euphrasia. Her father said she could, but it was so abominably bad that she simply could not help laughing, particularly at the hero in what was meant to be a tragic moment. He was terribly affronted but as Sarah was such a considerate girl he must have been irresistibly funny, or she would have controlled herself and not have laughed out loud.

Because they moved about so much the Kemble children had few chances of making outside friends, but there were so many of them, as well as the rest of the Company, that they had plenty of companionship. Sarah never went to any other school after Thornlea House, but Mr Kemble was always looking for any chance that came their way of giving her more education.

In the autumn of 1770 the Kembles moved to Brecon and stayed in The Shoulder of Mutton, the inn in which, just over fifteen years before Sarah had been born. They were there some time and it was here that Sarah began to realize that to many people she was no longer a child. Mr and Mrs Kemble might be blind to this, but the young men of Brecon were not. On the nights when she was singing or acting the theatre was full of them and they made it perfectly clear they had come mainly to see her and that they thought her quite unusually beautiful.

It was not only the young men of Brecon. William Siddons too began to realize that pretty, talented little Sarah Kemble was one of the loveliest girls he could ever hope to meet and that he had fallen deeply in love with her. He was intensely jealous of the young men who came to the theatre and particularly of a Mr Evans, a comparatively rich young man who owned an estate near by. Evans had come to the theatre by chance and heard Sarah sing 'Robin, Sweet Robin'. He was so impressed by this and with her beauty that he fell in love with her at once. It did not take him long to get to know her and from then on he haunted the theatre making it very plain, at least to Mr and Mrs Kemble and William, what his feelings were. To Sarah, strangely enough, it was not plain; she knew he liked her, but that was all. She was extraordinarily unaware of how beautiful she was and of how she impressed people. Because she was naturally modest and humble she did not realize that her looks, the way she carried her head and shoulders and her appearance of serene dignity would have been breath-taking in a far larger place than Brecon.

Mr and Mrs Kemble never wanted Sarah to make the stage her career – it was too precarious and had too many discomforts. The everlasting lodgings, often bad because good ones were too expensive, the slow and uncomfortable travelling, and the small salaries paid to actors made them hope that Sarah would marry and leave the stage. When, therefore, a country squire like Mr Evans came along, with a good house and a decent, though not large income, he seemed the answer to their hopes. They wanted Sarah to accept him and were prepared to give him all the help they could.

William Siddons saw all this and between love, despondency and jealousy was wretched. He could see quite clearly how his prospects looked compared with those of Evans. Sarah was not yet sixteen and but for Evans, William might have said nothing to her for some time, but because he was so jealous he could not keep his feelings to himself. Also, he felt that if her parents considered her old enough to have offers of marriage from other men they could not blame him for proposing. Summoning up his courage, he now did so.

Sarah had always liked him. William was tall, good-looking, kind and good, and when she realized he was in love with her, Evans did not stand a chance. She accepted William at once. She did not notice that he was not particularly intelligent, nor that he had not a very strong character, not even that he showed signs of pomposity, she just loved him. She had absolutely no doubt about this at all.

Even after she had accepted him, William was divided between hope and dark anxiety – what would Mr and Mrs Kemble say? He did not dare go to them and tell them he wanted to marry Sarah. There had been a short time when he believed they had guessed his feelings and were pleased with the idea, but he had since seen with dismay the encouragement they gave to Mr Evans. In a way he did not even wonder at this; parents could hardly be blamed if, having to choose between a strolling player of limited ability (William was always modest about his powers) and a young man of fortune and property, they chose the latter.

Mr Kemble was particularly anxious that Sarah should marry Evans, and he was furious when he discovered, as of course he did, that Sarah and William were engaged. Mrs Kemble had more sympathy with the lovers. She herself had married an actor in opposition to her father's wishes. She liked William – he had been with them a long time and had worked well, and she did not know much of Mr Evans. Her main feeling was that Sarah was too young to marry anyone at the moment – even too young to make up her mind whom she wanted to marry. She suggested that Sarah should make no promises to anyone, but should continue to see Mr Evans so that she could find out how much she liked him. She would, of course, at the same time continue to see William.

Sarah, who all her life hated scenes and unpleasantness, would have been happy to agree to this. She was sure she never would change her mind, but she agreed she was rather young to get married and sensibly felt that if it made things easier for everyone, William and she could wait a little. She was sure that when her parents saw that nothing would change them they would give their consent.

William was not at all prepared to do this. He did not feel sure that Sarah would not change her mind, there was so much against him; her parents' wishes, his poverty, and the fact that his rival was a young man with money. He begged Sarah to elope with him; if she would not, anything might happen to part them. But Sarah would not hear of an elopement. She knew it would hurt and upset her parents and felt it was quite unnecessary anyway because she was sure they would give in of their own accord before long. If only William would be quiet and trust her all would be perfectly well.

Quiet was just what William could not be. He made a scene so violent and uncontrolled that Mr and Mrs Kemble became involved in it. When they heard that he had proposed an elopement they were furious and in the general rising of tempers Mr Kemble gave him notice to quit his Company.

But exasperated as they were with him, Mr and Mrs Kemble felt sorry for William. He was a nice young man, although he was being foolish at the moment. Because they thought he might find it difficult to join another company at once and so would be short of money, they offered him a benefit night – that is a night on which most of the takings at the box-office would be given to him. Actors were so badly paid that it was the custom for them to have one or two benefit nights each season, to give them something over and above their salary. Farewell benefits were customary too, so Mr Kemble was not offering anything out of the ordinary, but in view of the quarrel they had had, William had not expected to get his.

On the benefit night the theatre was packed. Though the Kembles did not know it, everyone in Brecon was talking about Sarah Kemble and her love affairs and debating which one of her young men she would accept. As the Kembles were, on the whole, reserved, it had never crossed their minds that other people took so much interest in their private lives. William did know and made his plans accordingly.

On a benefit night it was usual for the person for whom it had been given to go down to the footlights when the play was over and make a speech to the audience. On this night William walked down as was expected, but instead of making a speech he said he was going to sing a song, the words of which he had written himself.

His stupidity is quite amazing. How he could have thought what he was about to do would endear him to the Kembles, or advance his cause one cannot imagine. He called his song *The Discarded Lover* and in it, in the most foolish and tactless way, told the story of his love for Sarah, claiming that she was false to him and making her parents sound cruel, simply because she had a richer lover. It was not a good song, as a song, and it put Mr and Mrs Kemble and Sarah in an odious light. It was not even true, as Sarah had never been false to him; she had only asked him to wait, maintaining that she would never stop loving him. He had no imagination or he would have realized how much they would dislike hearing themselves spoken of in verses like these :

'Ye ladies of Brecon, whose hearts ever feel
For wrongs like to this I'm about to reveal,
Excuse the first product, nor pass unregarded
The complaints of poor Colin, a lover discarded.

'Yet still on his Phyllis his hopes were all placed,
That her vows were so firm they could ne'er be effaced;
But soon she convinced him 't was all a mere joke,
For duty rose up, *and her vows were all broke.*

She acquainted her Ma'a, who, her ends to obtain,
Determined poor Colin to drive from the plain.

'Dear ladies, avoid one indelible stain,
Excuse me, I beg, if my verse is too plain;
But a jilt is the devil, as has long been confess'd,
Which a heart like poor Colin's must ever detest.'

The people of Brecon loved it. They had wanted to know what had really happened and now they thought they had been told. They sympathised with William and roared and applauded and clapped, and the applause went to William's head. He revelled in the sympathy and felt that he had stood up for himself bravely and no doubt made Sarah and her parents ashamed of their behaviour. But shame was not the emotion that filled Mrs Kemble; she was full of very natural fury. She was a tall woman and so could easily do what she wanted to do at that moment. As William came off the stage, she boxed his ears hard.

This was the beginning of another shattering scene. Exactly what everyone said is not known, but the situation finally sorted itself out by Sarah making William believe she did love him, even though she agreed to her parents' plan that she should leave the stage for a while and that William should leave the Company. She insisted that they should be allowed to write to each other, and even to see each other occasionally. Mr Kemble did not like this but agreed. He believed that Sarah would never remain in love with a man who had been so tactless and stupid and that when she was away from him she would come to her senses. He did not understand her at all. Though she was only fifteen she knew her own mind and having given her promise she was much too large-hearted, loving and loyal ever to go back on it. To comfort William she sent him some verses she had written. She was a better poet than he was and they express her feelings very faithfully :

'Say not, Strephon, I'm untrue,
When I only think of you :
If you do but think of me
As I of you, then shall you be
Without a rival in my heart,
Which ne'er can play a tyrant's part.

'Trust me, Strephon, with thy love —
I swear by Cupid's bow above,
Naught shall make me e'er betray
Thy passion till my dying day :
If I live, or if I die,
Upon my constancy rely.'

3 Interlude

After William left several changes took place in the family. Mr Kemble suddenly realized that he had three attractive young daughters (though Fanny and Elizabeth were only twelve and a half and ten) and decided that all three should have professions other than the stage. Sarah was sent to live with a family called Greatheed at their large country house, Guy's Cliffe (this, of course, had the additional advantage of taking her right out of William's way), Fanny was apprenticed to a milliner in Worcester, and Elizabeth to a dressmaker in Leominster. No protests from the girls (and Fanny and Elizabeth both hated the trades chosen for them) were listened to; their mother supported their father so away they all had to go.

Some time in the year 1771, Sarah was bowling along in a smart carriage nearer and nearer to her new post at Guy's Cliffe. She had travelled by stage-coach to Warwick, where she was met by the Greatheeds' carriage, and taken through the Warwickshire countryside to their large house in its wide grounds. The Kembles had never been friendly with any of the landed gentry so Sarah had never stayed in a great house before and arriving at such a place, to meet unknown employers was a terrible ordeal to a person as shy as she was.

As the servant announced her, Lady Mary Greatheed saw a tall, slender girl, who carried her head proudly and moved like a princess coming towards her. She dropped a stately curtsy and seemed perfectly self-possessed, but inside Sarah was fluttering with nervousness. Her new employer saw at once that she was most unusually beautiful.

Lady Mary was the daughter of the Duke of Ancaster and a delightful and friendly person and very soon Sarah was completely at home in Guy's Cliffe. She did not seem to have any definite duties. Bertie Greatheed, Lady Mary's son who was about twelve when Sarah first went to them, years afterwards said she had been engaged as a maid to his mother for a salary of £10 a year, but she was certainly never treated like a servant. She became one of the family immediately and her only duties seem to have been reading aloud, chiefly Shakespeare and Milton. Otherwise she was free to do what she liked and to roam about the house and the lovely gardens and the grounds that went right down to the banks of the river Avon.

Living in a beautiful house with rich people was a completely new experience for Sarah and she loved it. It gave her a taste for comfort and elegance she never lost. Although all her life she could put up with unavoidable discomfort, whenever she could have lovely things about her she did. The contrast between her old life and her new could hardly have been greater; staying in one place instead of for ever moving about, living in an expensively furnished house instead of lodging in inexpensive inns, and spending long hours of idleness instead of being involved in the constant bustle of activity on and behind the stage.

Sarah was happy at the Greatheeds, but all the luxury and elegance did not make her give up her determination to be an actress and she often acted to herself or to the servants. Even when she went with Lady Mary to stay with the Dowager Duchess of Ancaster, in Lincolnshire, she could not resist using some of the great empty rooms as a stage and if she could get an audience she was delighted. Lady Mary's brother, Lord Robert Bertie, was tremendously impressed with her. He heard her giving a recitation in the servants' hall and raved about her to his sister. Lady Mary agreed that she was remarkably good – she had a way of making poetry come alive that was a great gift. They had all noticed that when she read *Paradise Lost* aloud everyone had to listen, but in spite of this Lady Mary hoped no one would encourage her to be an actress. She knew Mr Kemble was very much against it. And no wonder. The life of a travelling player was very hard for anyone, let alone a young woman; it would be far better if Sarah married. As she was so beautiful there was every likelihood that she would, and marry well. She would grace any walk of life. She was so queenly in her movements that Lady Mary herself felt an almost irresistible desire to get up from her chair every time Sarah came into the room.

Although they had not been forbidden to meet it was almost impossible for William to get to Guy's Cliffe, the journey was too expensive, but he and Sarah corresponded regularly. Sarah had few visits from her family. Her parents could not afford the journey either, and there was no chance of John coming because when he left Sedgerly Park he went to Douai, the Roman Catholic Seminary on the Continent, where he was to train for the priesthood.

While she was at the Greatheeds Sarah saw David Garrick for the first time and had an audition with him. He was considered by everyone in England as incomparably the greatest actor on the English stage and this must have been a tremendous moment for her. Garrick was coming towards the end of his wonderful career. For over thirty years he had thrilled audiences. Many people believed, with his more natural style, he was the greatest actor England had ever had. Since Shakespeare's day, and for many years before Garrick joined the theatre, actors believed in speaking their lines – almost all plays were written in blank verse – beautifully and rhetorically, but with no attempt to make them natural. Their movements, too, were stilted and conventional and their gestures had become stereotyped and very exaggerated; they clasped their hands and rolled their eyes and struck their foreheads to express their emotions. They stalked instead of walking and their speaking often became mere ranting. David Garrick changed all this. He believed that more natural acting made a far greater impact on an audience and his popularity proved that he was right. He was equally good in comedy or tragedy. He was so immeasurably the greatest man on the stage that it was a wonder that Sarah had the courage to ask for an audition. But William, who all his life had boundless belief in her ability as an actress, encouraged her to do so and it shows what her career meant to her that she was able to overcome her shyness.

Garrick was a little man, shorter than Sarah herself, but his superb self-confidence and his great reputation was enough to overawe any girl appearing before him. Sarah chose the part of Jane Shore for her audition, from a play of that name which was very popular at the time. It is a play about the wife of a rich City of London merchant who becomes the mistress of King Edward iv. After the King's death the play is about her deep repentance, the inhuman way in which she is treated by most people, including Richard iii, and her final death from starvation. On the whole Sarah preferred tragedy to comedy and as Jane Shore was one of the famous tragedy parts of the day she thought it a good choice, but it was not a wise one because she had no experience of such a person.

She did not do herself justice and Garrick was not particularly impressed with her performance. He was quite kind and praised her for the way she walked and carried herself, and thought she spoke well. He wondered how she had managed to get rid of the 'Provincial ti-tum-ti' in her speech, but he regretted that he could do nothing for her. He tried to soften the blow by explaining why he could not engage her to play in his Company – he had all the actresses he could use, Miss Younge, Mrs Yates and Mrs Abington, to say nothing of Miss Hopkins and Mrs King. No doubt if he had been immensely impressed he would have fitted her in somehow, but like many another manager looking for talent, he was taken with her beauty and youth, but was sure she could not take the place of any of his leading ladies and did not think she had enough talent to make it worth engaging her. So he thanked her for her audition and wished her good morning.

Sarah said nothing to anyone about this rebuff, but it did not alter her determination to make the stage her career. It was a blow to her pride, but her self-confidence was not too badly shaken. She still meant to act, even if she had to content herself with success in the provinces without aspiring to London fame.

4 Back to the Boards

Sarah was with the Greatheeds for about two years before she persuaded her parents to let her return to them and to the theatre. She also made Mr and Mrs Kemble agree to her marriage, for although she and William had been parted all this time, they were more sure than ever of their love for each other. Sarah knew she could not be happy without her parents' consent, but she did not see how they could refuse it any longer, because they could no longer say she and William did not know their own minds. She was now eighteen and William was nearly thirty and if a man did not know his own mind at that age he never would. They had proved their love was real and there was no reason why they should not get married.

Although Mr and Mrs Kemble had wanted her to go to the Greatheeds to separate her from the stage, they were glad to have her back for many reasons. Mrs Kemble only had nine-year-old Anne at home to help her and she was expecting another baby during the winter. As Sarah was as keen on the stage as ever and the experiment of turning her into a young lady of leisure had failed, they were thankful to have her to help at home and play the juvenile leads.

The Greatheeds were sorry to part with her and in some ways she was sorry to go. Her years at Guy's Cliffe had given her, besides lifelong friends, a greatly increased appreciation of beauty, elegance and culture, and had broadened her mind and made her at ease in society. Lady Mary gave her a beautifully bound edition of Milton's works as a parting present, just the sort of thing Sarah appreciated.

Her parents were at Coventry when she rejoined them, and she fell back into the old life with relish, with no apparent regrets for the comfort and luxury she had become used to. The orderly, leisurely life had done her health good and she was full of energy, and becoming more beautiful every day. Mr and Mrs Kemble could not help being very proud of her. They congratulated themselves on having sent her to the Greatheeds. Even if she had insisted on being an actress after all, life at Guy's Cliffe had made her into a very graceful and well-mannered young lady.

But leisure and comfort and even being an elegant young woman was not what Sarah really cared about. She wanted first, last and all the time to be an actress and so long as it was connected with the theatre she did not mind what she did – playing big or small parts, making costumes or being noises off. She was delighted to be at home again and showed all her old sweetness and sense of fun. She usually saw the funny side of things and could put up with discomforts gaily and turn her hand to anything – nursing the new baby when it came, darning, ironing, anything that was wanted.

Immediately she arrived home Mr and Mrs Kemble began to realize that parting her from William had been useless and that she was still determined to marry him. Mr Kemble would have held out for a bit longer, but his wife was sure that William was again trying to persuade Sarah to elope to Gretna Green and believed that if they continued to say no she might. She made her husband see the real danger of this, so that quite suddenly he gave way completely. Not only could Sarah marry William, he would give her away and he would re-engage William to play in his Company. Mr Kemble's Company of Comedians would become a family affair once more.

William was a bit bewildered by this sudden change in his fortunes, but there were no hard feelings because of the past and he was delighted to come back.

They had a very quiet wedding. There was not much money to waste on festivities and Mrs Kemble, who was only a month off her tenth confinement, certainly did not want to organize a large wedding party. Sarah and William walked to Holy Trinity Church, Coventry, on the morning of 26 November 1773 and were married by the curate.

They had no honeymoon – their engagements with the theatre would not let them be away, even if they could have raised the money. Mr Kemble's Company was due to leave Coventry and go to Leominster immediately – two, if not three days' journey by their old coach – and then had to go on to Wolverhampton, which would take nearly as long. Mr Kemble was having difficulty in getting a licence to act in the latter town. The Mayor was so violently against theatrical people that he had announced that 'neither player, puppy nor monkey' should perform in Wolverhampton. Luckily for the Kembles the townspeople rebelled at this and forced the Mayor to change his mind, so that they were able to put on their plays.

Two were advertised on 13 December – *The West Indian* in which Sarah played Charlotte Rusport, and *The Padlock* when she played the heroine, Leonora. It was her own 'bespeak' or benefit night, and it was the first time she was billed under the name she was to make so famous – Mrs Siddons.

As usual Sarah had to say something at the end of her benefit, and she and William wrote some verses for her to speak. From the quality of them it looks as if they mostly came from William's brain, because they have a strong likeness to his Brecon effort.

> 'Ladies and Gentlemen – my spouse and I,
> Have had a squabble, and I'll tell you why —
> He said I must appear; nay vowed it right,
> To give you thanks for favours shown tonight.

> 'He still insisted, and to win consent,
> Strove to o'ercome me with a compliment;
> Told me that I the favourite here had reigned,
> While he but small or no applause had gained.'

Poor William. This was a very prophetic remark because it was always going to be Sarah who was the favourite, and for whom the applause would sound. She ended with a reference to her father, and a general good wish for Wolverhampton.

> 'First for a father, who on this fair ground
> Has met with friendship seldom to be found,
> May th' All-good Power your every virtue nourish,
> Health, wealth and trade in Wolverhampton flourish!'

Even in an age when audiences expected such things, Sarah's talent must have been considerable to get this sort of doggerel across.

For the rest of the winter Sarah and William played in the Kembles' Company. It was a hard life; money was extremely scarce, largely because of the competition from other companies on the same circuit. People enjoyed going to the theatre, but few could afford to go very often and some of the productions by other companies were so bad they put audiences off altogether. In consequence the Kembles often played to half-empty houses. Sometimes, too, when they got to a town they could not get a licence to act, which meant the whole venture was a total loss. As always they were not fussy where they performed, and Sarah acted again in inn yards, in halls, in tumbledown theatres and barns as she had done so many times. Nothing could have been a greater contrast to the Greatheeds' beautiful home and ordered life, but she and William were blissfully happy together and thoroughly enjoyed the hard work and regretted nothing.

Mrs Kemble acted very little that winter. On 29 December when they were in Leominster, she had another little boy, Henry, and as he was a delicate child she could not leave him to take part in any of the plays.

While they were at Leominster they saw as much as possible of Elizabeth, who certainly was not made more satisfied with her trade of millinery when she saw Sarah acting. Mr Kemble's attempts to make his girls give up the stage failed with her and Fanny just as it had with Sarah, because as soon as their apprenticeships were over they both returned to the stage.

The Kembles' Company made so little money that winter that both Sarah and William wondered if they ought not to try to get into a more prosperous one, and when Sarah found she was going to have a baby they considered it even more seriously. On the one hand it seemed unkind to leave Mr Kemble, on the other they had to make enough money to support a family. The suggestion was made tentatively and Sarah's parents agreed to it without any ill-will or hard feelings, sorry as they were to part with such a splendid pair of workers. Even William was a great deal better than many they had to choose from, while Sarah was irreplaceable.

The problem was which company to join, and when William negotiated with the partners Chamberlain and Crump, and agreed to play for them, Sarah was doubtful if he had done wisely. They had the reputation of being mean and tyrannical and she thought their nicknames, Fox and Bruin, very sinister. William, however, mantained doggedly he was sure he was right. Chamberlain and Crump had offered steady, though small salaries and had promised Sarah good parts. They knew their business and anyway, the matter was settled now. This being so there was no point in making any more fuss, and in the spring they joined Chamberlain and Crump.

Sarah was proved only too right about them. The change did not bring the Siddonses much more money and the work was even harder. They were always on the move, sometimes playing for only one night, and then on again next day by stage-coach or in the uncomfortable, springless old coach provided by Messrs Fox and Bruin. The inns varied, but Sarah and William could only afford the cheaper rooms and at every stop they had to play long, emotional parts, probably a different one every day. It was lucky they were young and strong and in love and could put up with it.

They played at Cheltenham during the summer. This town, though still small, was becoming fashionable as a watering place. Its one long street was clean and well-paved, and had the unusual attraction of a little, swift-running, clear stream through it, bridged at intervals by stepping stones. Though the town was pleasant the theatre was much less so, being very shabby and dirty. Of course it was the only theatre in the town so all travelling companies, good, bad and indifferent had to use it and Chamberlain and Crump brought their company there to play for as long as they could get audiences.

One of the plays they put on was Thomas Otway's *Venice Preserved*, in which Sarah had the tremendous part of the heroine, Belvidera, who finally goes mad at the end of the play. It was the kind of part Sarah enjoyed – she always loved great tragedy even when she played to unsophisticated, bucolic audiences, and in Cheltenham, now that it was becoming fashionable, there might be a few better educated people who could appreciate good acting when they saw it.

The ticket manager was delighted when one day a party of just such people took tickets for the performance that night. It was soon buzzing round backstage who they were – Lord Bruce and his wife and step-daughter, the Hon. Henrietta Boyle. The last-named had actually written poetry and had had one poem at least – 'An Ode to a Poppy' – published.

The whole company was cheered and thrilled by the excitement of acting to such people, and to Sarah, sitting in her wretched dressing-room (although she was the leading lady this was only a bit of the wings screened off by an old blanket) it was like a breath of life. Then word began to go round that Lord Bruce and his party were only coming to jeer. They had seen the bills advertising *Venice Preserved* by chance as they passed the theatre, and had decided to come to see, and laugh at, the hash a second-rate provincial company made of it.

Some tactless person told Sarah this just before she went on, and the excitement she had felt before made her feel doubly depressed now she knew the truth. She also felt deeply resentful of people who came only to scoff. Did they suppose that any player chose a second-rate company to act with, or pokey, dirty theatres to act in for preference? As she walked forward on to the stage she felt more despairing and despondent about her career than she had ever done before.

It was one of the conventions in the theatre of the eighteenth century for actors to wait for applause after any telling speech, and then nod and bow to the audience to acknowledge it. Sarah never did this – she was always too absorbed in her part even to look at the auditorium. She could not come out of character, bow and smirk to the audience, and then go back into character again. This particular night the box in which these horrible, jeering people were sitting was so close to the stage that she could not ignore its occupants completely, and the muffled sounds that came from them nearly drove her distracted. She was so strung up and so full of resentment that she stormed through the part, trying, but failing, to shut her mind to the insulting, wounding behaviour of these cruel critics. The moment the play was over she went home, bitterly mortified, and deeply depressed and despondent about the future.

William's pride was nearly as outraged as hers, and he was still in a very ruffled mood when he saw Lord Bruce coming down the street towards him next day. Although he hardly expected that Lord Bruce would recognize him, he prepared to stalk past him with his head in the air. To his surprise his lordship stopped him and the moment he began to speak William realized just how mistaken he and Sarah had been. Lady Bruce and Miss Boyle had not been laughing at Sarah, they had been crying. They had been so overcome and carried away by her acting that the noises they made came from suppressed sobs, not laughter. Not only that, but Sarah's wonderful portrayal of Belvidera's suffering had so upset them that they had not been able to sleep all night and both had violent headaches that morning. But for that they would have been round already to tell Mrs Siddons how marvellous they thought she was. When William grasped what Lord Bruce was saying he could hardly stay to be civil he was so anxious to get back to tell Sarah.

She could hardly believe him. When she did her spirits soared nearly as high as they had sunk before. She was naturally a buoyant person, but she had needed a tonic like this to renew her confidence in herself.

As soon as Miss Boyle recovered from her headache she hurried round to the rather dismal lodgings which were all the Siddonses could afford. The sight of Sarah's surroundings made her realize that an actress could do with more concrete help than just admiration, and she very soon found out just how hard the pair were finding life. Miss Boyle was a delightful person, pretty, intelligent and so genuinely friendly that Sarah found herself admitting, as to an old friend, that one of her main difficulties was in finding the right clothes for her parts, she had so little money to spend on them. Leading players usually provided their own costumes (those provided by the management were mostly so dirty and shabby that they were useless) and this was a heavy expense. Queens and grand ladies had to be dressed reasonably well, and clothes cost a lot of money.

Miss Boyle was well-to-do and delighted to help. She gave Sarah dresses of her own, expensive materials which she helped to make up, and shawls, lace and ornaments as well. She was so tactful in the way she did this that Sarah was able to take everything without embarrassment. Almost best of all was to make such a real friend.

Sarah thoroughly enjoyed this season in Cheltenham; it made such a difference to have a really intelligent family in the audience. The Bruces came to nearly every play Sarah was in. On one occasion one of their party even lent her his coat when she had to wear a man's clothes in the part of the Widow Brady. He stood in the wings with her petticoat over his shoulders while she went on in his coat. An episode of this sort gives some idea how disorganized, amateur and haphazard even professional companies were in the eighteenth century. Imagine today even an amateur company of any standing presenting a play without making sure that the leading lady had a costume to wear for it, and having to borrow one from a member of the audience at the last moment!

Lord Bruce also tried to help Sarah more permanently. He knew Garrick well and told him about this wonderful young actress they had discovered playing at Cheltenham. Garrick was interested, but did not connect this find with the beautiful girl he had seen at the Greatheeds. As her surname was changed there was no reason why he should. He was enough impressed with Lord Bruce's enthusiasm to send Mr King, one of his own, well-known actors, to see Sarah act, but he did not tell anyone he was doing so, and no one in Cheltenham had any idea Mr King was coming. No one even knew he came. He slipped into the theatre without being recognized, and slipped away afterwards; Sarah only learned about it much later.

Mr King saw her in a play called *The Fair Penitant*. She played the part of the heroine, Calista, and he was immensely impressed. He went back to London and told Garrick that she was quite remarkably beautiful and that her acting was simple and yet so expressive that it had tremendous power to move audiences. He strongly advised Garrick to engage her.

Garrick, however, still hesitated. He knew perfectly well that his three main actresses (still Miss Younge, Mrs Yates and Mrs Abington) would not be able to hold audiences for ever, and that he would have to look for a younger, new actress before long, but he did not think the moment had yet come. He was not really frightened that anyone else would snap this Siddons woman up, and for the moment he decided just to keep an eye on her and only when he thought the time was ripe to offer her a part in his company. There was no hurry, he felt, and a little more experience in the provinces could do her no harm.

Sarah and William, of course, knew nothing of this and went on playing for Chamberlain and Crump. Sarah, in fact, acted right up to the time when, on 4 October, their first child, a boy whom they called Henry, was born at Wolverhampton. His first experiences were just what Sarah's own had been; he was bundled about from town to town, nursed at the back of draughty stages, and put to sleep in dressing-rooms that were no more than curtained-off recesses in the wings, and it did him no more harm than it had done her. But his birth did make his parents even more anxious to succeed on the stage than they had ever been before.

5 London Scene

In spite of the Cheltenham interlude Sarah and William were not happy with Chamberlain and Crump, who paid badly and worked their players unreasonably hard. Now that they had Henry to think of as well, they decided to leave when they could. When the opportunity arose to join Mr Younger's Company early in the spring of 1775 they took it gladly.

It was some time in the spring or early summer of this year that Sarah first met a little boy who, when he was grown up, was to play a very important part in the life of the Siddons family. It happened when she and William were staying at The Bear Inn in Devizes. The landlord was a man called Lawrence, a rolling stone who had been an attorney's clerk, an actor, an exciseman and was now trying to make some money as an innkeeper. One evening, just before she went to the theatre, Sarah was sitting in the sitting-room of the inn when the innkeeper's eldest child, Thomas, an unusually handsome little boy, came into the room, riding a hobby-horse. He was only about six but not at all shy, and he came up and stood looking at her. Sarah took to him at once; later she found that he was not only lively, intelligent and good-looking, but extraordinarily gifted too. Although he was such a little boy he could draw remarkable likenesses of people; he is supposed to have done one of her, though unfortunately it is lost. He made a drawing of Lord Kenyon which Lady Kenyon said was the best likeness ever made of him. Besides being a draughtsman, little Thomas Lawrence could recite great passages of Shakespeare and Milton by heart. He was often called for in the bar, and when he appeared someone would pick up the little boy with his beautiful sensitive face and huge eyes and put him on the counter, where he would stand reciting to the men around.

The Siddonses found Mr Younger's Company far more pleasant than Chamberlain and Crump's. Sarah began to make a name for herself throughout all the western counties and she and William thought they saw a successful career in the provinces opening up before them. They had no idea that Garrick had ever been interested in Sarah, still less that he was keeping her in mind, and that he had written to an actor called Moody, then playing at Liverpool, asking, 'Have you heard of a woman Siddons who is strolling about somewhere near you?'

Younger's Company had just come to Liverpool, so Moody located Sarah at once and went to see her act. His reports were so favourable that in August Garrick sent the Rev Mr Henry Bate, a hearty, bluff parson who was far more interested in the theatre than in his work as a priest, to report on Sarah, who was again playing at Cheltenham.

After combatting the various difficulties of one of the cussidest cross-roads in this kingdom' Mr Bate and his wife arrived at Cheltenham and betook themselves to the theatre. They saw Sarah as Rosalind in *As You Like It*. At that moment she was only four months off having another baby, so it seems strange that she was playing Rosalind who spends so much of the play disguised as a boy, even if it was one of her favourite parts. For some reason Younger's Company was not acting in the theatre, but in a barn, with a stage only nine feet wide. Mr Bate (perhaps he could not get a seat) did not even see the play from the front; he stood in the wings and watched. Sarah made a very great impression on him. 'Her face,' he wrote to Garrick, 'is one of the most strikingly beautiful for stage effect that I ever beheld,' and he thought even her beauty less remarkable than her acting, which had more variety, and was more natural than that of any other actress he had ever seen. He thought her particularly good in the comedy parts, and said of one scene that 'she did more with it than anyone I ever saw, not even . . . divine Mrs Barry excepted.'

The only adverse comment he made was about Sarah's voice, which he said he thought was a little grating, though he admitted that this wore off as the play wore on, and as no one else ever remarked on this, it was either his imagination or something quite temporary. He was particularly impressed by her naturalness and the fact that, though she had been on the stage from a child, acting in inferior companies, she had not picked up any of the bad habits and tricks which so often ruined the performance of strolling players.

Mr Bate was so enthusiastic that he followed Mr Younger's players to Worcester, where he put up at The Hop Pole. He wrote again to Garrick from there saying that though he had so far only seen her in one play he believed she would be equally good in any part and that he thought the present Drury Lane actresses would have good reason to be jealous of her. He even warned Garrick to beware of his laurels, as Sarah had played 'Hamlet to the satisfaction of the Worcester critics!'

While he was in Worcester Mr Bate learned that some of the Covent Garden talent spotters – he called them Mohawks – 'were entrenched near the place and intended carrying her (Sarah) by surprise'. There were only two licensed theatres in London in those days, Covent Garden and Drury Lane, and naturally Mr Bate was not going to let Drury Lane's great rival get their hands on this marvellous actress if he could help it. He lost no time and although he told Garrick that William Siddons was 'a damned rascally player' he knew he could not have Sarah without him, and he wrote to William at once, telling him he wanted to see him and his wife, and why.

Sarah and William were completely taken by surprise by this letter; they had no idea that an offer from Drury Lane was within their reach. They were thrilled and exalted and only too willing to agree to any terms Mr Bate might suggest. He, for his part, was extremely pleased with the modesty and diffidence the Siddonses showed; they were very different from the arrogant players he had known, though he wondered how long Sarah would retain her modesty and diffidence once she got to London.

He wrote to Garrick that he would see Sarah in as many plays as he could, and if he altered his opinion about her he would let him know, but both he and his wife felt pretty confident that he had discovered a real genius. 'I shall expect to hear from you by return of post,' he ended, 'as Siddons will call upon me to know whether you look upon her as engaged.'

Garrick was interested enough to answer by return as asked. He wrote from his house in Hampton, on 15 August. 'Ten thousand thanks for your very clear, agreeable and friendly letter,' he wrote. '. . . I must desire you to secure the lady, with my best compliments.'

From the first Garrick was interested only in Sarah, though he realized he would have to engage William too. After Mr Bate's unflattering remarks of William's playing Garrick made it very clear that he was not offering William good parts – some sort of back stage work or tiny parts were all that he could expect. Bate's next letter, however, was slightly more flattering to William. 'He is much more tolerable than I thought him at first,' he wrote. 'I saw him the other evening in Young Marlow, in Goldsmith's comedy, and then he was far from despicable; neither his figure nor face contemptible.' Considering that William was tall and handsome this is hardly high praise, especially from a man as determined to see good in the Siddonses as Mr Bate, but it is better than being called a 'rascally player'. Every time Mr Bate saw Sarah he was more enthusiastic about her.

In spite of all this the negotiations were not settled immediately. Younger did not want to part with Sarah, Covent Garden said she had engaged herself to them, and as Sarah could not start in Drury Lane until after her baby was born she and William were afraid at one time that they would fall between all these stools. They were never grasping about terms and were perfectly ready to accept anything Garrick thought fair, but they were anxious to know if he would pay them while they were waiting to join his company, and they also wanted to know what sort of salary William would have. In the end it was fixed that they were to go to Drury Lane after Sarah's baby was born and that Garrick should give them £20 to see them through any expenses they might have till then.

Garrick never saw Sarah once through all these negotiations; he relied entirely on Bate's judgement, but she could not have had a more eager advocate. He kept on stressing not only her superlative good looks and her acting ability, but also the good characters she and William had both on and off the stage. He also wrote, 'She [Sarah] is the most extraordinary quick study I ever heard of. This cannot be amiss, for, if I recollect right, we have a sufficient number of leaden-headed ones at D. Lane already.'

Delighted as the Siddonses were to be going to Drury Lane, they were not going to be much richer. Sarah was to get £3 and William £2 a week. (Before long Sarah got paid the whole £5 and William's engagement just lapsed.) Any benefit performances would be worth a great deal more in London, of course, but they both felt that the main thing was that Sarah should have a chance of showing what a wonderful actress she was to audiences that could apppreciate her.

Sarah's baby daughter came earlier than was expected, and she was acting right up to the time that her baby was born on

5 November at Gloucester. They christened this daughter Sarah Martha and always called her Sally.

Although travelling for everyone in those days, even the rich, was slow and usually uncomfortable, Sarah was never one to anticipate difficulties; she was always hopeful. But even she might have hesitated before taking her place in Garrick's Company while she was still not perfectly recovered from the birth of her baby, especially when this involved a long coach journey in the middle of winter. None of this worried her at all – she was only concerned that she had missed the first two months of the Drury Lane season. Theatre seasons in London always opened in September and went on till the late spring or early summer in the next year. The theatres, or the two big ones, were always closed through the summer months.

Sally Siddons was not the only child born to the Kemble family this winter. Mrs Kemble had her twelfth and last child, a boy whom they called Charles. Like Sarah he was born at Brecon and, like her too, he was to make a great name for himself on the stage, though he was never as famous as his brilliant sister.

It took the Siddonses five days to get from Gloucester to London that December. The normal stage between inns varied between seven to twelve miles, and might take from one to two hours, depending on the weather and the state of the road. The coaches were all unwarmed and one either sat on the top, and was cold and windblown (or soaked if it was raining or snowing) or sat inside which was cold and stuffy. There was straw on the floor inside, meant to keep people's feet warm, but passengers usually got so chilled that they were thankful for the many stops at inns where they could thaw out and get something to eat. The roads on the whole were terrible, full of huge pot-holes and stretches of mud in which it was quite normal for coaches to get stuck, and from which they were hauled with difficulty.

The whole enterprise was rather alarming to country people like Sarah and William because, though they were perfectly used to travelling, they were not used to a town the size of London, with its streets jammed full of carts, coaches, drays, chaises and curricles so that the noise of the clatter of hoofs and the untyred wheels on the cobbles was deafening. The enormous size of the place was daunting. But no dreary journey and no alarm at the vastness and bustle of London could alter one fact for Sarah. Her great opportunity had come; she was going to act in the most famous theatre in London and with the most famous actor, and at his request.

If London seemed overwhelming, so did Drury Lane when Sarah, trembling with nervousness, first went into it. It was to her unbelievably large. The distant gallery of 'the gods', the highest circle of seats, looked almost out of sight, and below were tier upon tier of boxes, divided from each other by elegant pillars of white and gold. She was astonished at its beauty, too, after the scruffy barns and playhouses to which she was used. Adams had painted the ceiling and the gilt and plush and the chandeliers in the auditorium were magnificent. The stage could be more brilliantly lit than any she had ever been on. Not only were the lamps in the footlights brighter than smoky candles, but Garrick had introduced lamps in the wings, each one of which could be dimmed by a shutter. These were fixed to ladders in tiers, and could send strong beams of light from the wings on to the acting area, while above the stage were a number of chandeliers. She was impressed too by the dressing-rooms – real rooms with furniture and mirrors and by the space both on the stage and behind it.

The size of the theatre was not the only thing to overwhelm her; the players were even more intimidating. The leading actresses stared at her coldly. They were not at all anxious to welcome to their number a particularly beautiful young woman, reputed to be an outstandingly good actress. Sarah was made to feel this at once. Mrs Yates, Miss Younge and Mrs Abington were a terrifying trio to a young, nervous, diffident provincial actress. Mrs Yates, who played the tragedy parts, was tall, good-looking and majestic. Her figure was large; unkind people said too large just as they said her beautiful voice was monotonous. Miss Younge was younger and had far more animation. She was tall too, but slender. Mrs Abington was the comedy actress and was less jealous of Sarah than the others. Besides the stars there were Miss Hopkins, the prompter's daughter and Mrs King, both pretty young women who played the smaller parts.

All theatres in those days were run somewhat like a repertory theatre is now. A permanent company was kept together for a season or seasons, and each member would have, by and large, his or her type of part. Although they tried out new plays, for a lot of the time they acted old favourites.

Although the leading ladies cold-shouldered her, Garrick went out of his way to be kind, making her sit beside him and putting her into his box so that she could watch rehearsals. He decided that her first appearance should be as Portia in *The Merchant of Venice*. She was not billed by name at all – she simply appeared on the posters as 'A Young Lady'. Bracketed after this were the words, 'her first appearance'.

Poor Sarah. Far from taking London by storm, as she had imagined herself doing, she was, quite simply, a flop. She was terribly nervous, the brilliant lighting upset her, and she knew that her clothes (a faded salmon-pink sack and coat) were hideous and most unbecoming to her, and she had not really got over Sally's birth. She literally tottered on to the stage and spoke so low that no one could hear her. She did pull herself together by the time she came to the trial scene and gave an intelligent rendering of the part, but even then she kept dropping her voice. It was a miserable evening and the papers next day made it quite clear what they thought of her performance. One said, 'On before us tottered rather than walked, a very pretty, delicate, fragile-looking young creature, dressed in a most unbecoming manner, in a faded salmon-coloured sack and coat, and uncertain whereabouts to fix either her eyes or her feet. She spoke in broken, tremulous tones; and at the close of a sentence her words generally lapsed into a horrid whisper, that was absolutely inaudible. After her first exit, the judgement of the pit was unanimous as to her beauty, but declared her awkward and provincial.'

It was agreed that in the trial scene she was more at ease, but even then she was hard to hear. 'Altogether the impression made upon the audience by this first effort was of the most negative nature.' Another paper said that 'they understood that the new Portia had been the heroine of one of those petty parties of travelling comedians which wander over the country' and seemed to think it a pity that she had ever left them. They did admit that she had a fine stage figure; that her 'features were expressive'; and that she was 'uncommonly graceful'; but said that her voice was 'deficient in tone and clearness', although this might have been due to nervousness. They agreed that her words were spoken with good sense, but there was no fire or spirit in her performance.

Sarah was terribly depressed by these criticisms. She realized only too well they were true, but could not think why. After the notices she was used to getting, it was difficult for her to believe it was she of whom the papers were speaking. She never quite grasped why she failed in her first season in London. She came to believe afterwards that it was Garrick's fault; she felt he had not pushed her enough. But this is certainly untrue. He did as much as could be expected and was very kind to her. Perhaps he could have protected her more from the sneers and jealousies of his Company, though it is hard to know what exactly he could have done, since any kindness to her simply aggravated things. He probably felt too, that this was just one of the things players had to get used to. Sarah anyway was not giving such good performances that she merited good parts, though Garrick did offer her Venus in his Jubilee pageant.

Before this performance was over, Sarah heartily wished he had not. She was no doubt given it because she was so beautiful (she had nothing to say in it) and this made the other actresses furious. No one found fault with his choice to Garrick's face, but everyone vented their spite on Sarah. As she afterwards said, 'The fulsome adulation that courted Garrick in the theatre cannot be imagined; and whosoever the luckless wight who should be honoured by his distinguished and envied smiles, of course became the object of spite and malevolence.'

She did not only have to endure sneers. On the first night of the Pageant, Venus and Cupid were very nearly mobbed by the other players. They were supposed to come down to the front of the stage but the rest of the cast quite deliberately crowded round them to prevent this – they would almost in fact have been pushed into the wings if Garrick had not intervened. Sarah was hopeless at coping with this sort of behaviour – she could not jostle and shove people to get into her proper place. Garrick, however, saw at once what was happening and was quite able to deal with the situation. He very soon cleared a way for her and, taking her by the hand, led her and Cupid down to their proper places.

Cupid was a boy called Thomas Dibdin. He was supposed to appear smiling and jovial and to keep on looking so, but on this first night he was so alarmed by this episode – he was only about seven and had nearly been knocked over – that he was much nearer tears than smiles. Sarah, with great presence of mind, even in the midst of her own misery, immediately asked him what kind of sugar plums he liked best, and promised him a good supply of them when they came off the stage if he would only keep on smiling and try to look as if he were enjoying himself. Thomas managed to do this and after making her dignified retreat to her dressing-room through the hostile groups of the other players, Sarah immediately sent out for the sugar plums. Thomas Dibdin loved her dearly. When he was sick one day and another boy had to take his part, he was distractedly jealous of him. 'I could have killed that boy,' he wrote afterwards, but he was appeased on his return to the stage by Sarah saying to him, 'I did not like Master Mills half so well as I do you.'

The Venus episode naturally did not make Sarah any more popular, and she was worried when several days went by without a part being offered to her. Then on 13 January 1776, Garrick told her she was to play a small part in Ben Jonson's *Epicoene*, principally because of her good 'breeches figure' as she had to wear boy's clothes. Following that he gave her another small part in an opera by the Henry Bate who was responsible for getting her to Drury Lane. The opera (probably what we should call a musical) was *The Blackamoor Washed White* and was quite deplorably bad. Garrick, to oblige his friend, staged it with all the elaborate scenery he could – 'Lawns, lodges and avenues', but the audience would have none of it and did not hesitate to say so.

No audience in those days saw any need to be polite to actors or playwrights. If they did not like a play they made this perfectly clear. They did not like *The Blackamoor Washed White* and on the third night it was shown there was a riot. People shouted and threw things on to the stage and then half the audience started fighting among themselves, while terrified ladies tried to get out, much handicapped by their huge hooped dresses. When Garrick tried to make himself heard, he had an orange thrown at him, and later someone threw a lighted candle on to the stage. It was almost midnight before the riot died down and then it only did so because Garrick promised to take the play off and never put it on again.

6   Back to the Provinces

Riots of that kind are unnerving for any player and the scenes in Drury Lane did not make Sarah feel more confident, and her notices for *The Blackamoor Washed White* were bad. Actually there had been so much noise and shouting that she had not been able to make herself heard and under such conditions it was impossible for anyone to judge her performance, but all the papers did so. One said, 'Mrs Siddons, having no comedy in her nature, rendered ridiculous that which the author evidently intended to be pleasant.' For Sarah, whom Bate had thought so good in comedy parts, this was very disheartening.

She was very unhappy. It was all so different from what she had expected. She had never had notices like this before and Mr Garrick seemed in no hurry to give her a chance to show people what she could do. Years and years later, when she was an old woman, she said that Garrick had told her he could not give her prominent parts, however good she was, because if he did the other actresses would have poisoned her, and she agreed there was something in it. She did not really believe that they would have murdered her, but Miss Younge and Mrs Yates were so jealous and so uncontrolled in their behaviour that she would have had to put up with an incredible amount of ill-will and malice. She had quite enough of that as it was.

Garrick, of course, was not really holding her back and four days later he gave her quite a good part in a comedy called *The Runaway*, which had a long run for those days – it was put on for seventeen consecutive nights. And when that was over he let her play opposite him as Mrs Strickland in a play called *The Suspicious Husband*.

Neither of these parts was exciting – both nervous and timid women – and because she longed to show people what she could do in some great tragic role like Belvidera, Sarah was still dissatisfied. She was a little cheered, however, to see her name in quite big print on the posters for *The Suspicious Husband*.

Sarah was a bundle of nerves when she went on to the stage for the opening night of *The Suspicious Husband*. It was the first time she had played with Garrick and she had heard enough about his acting to be very nervous. He was so realistic that even the players themselves found it impossible sometimes to remember that he was acting. Once, in *Macbeth*, when he said to one of the murderers, 'There's blood upon thy face', the man not only thought there really was and tried to wipe it off, but felt as if he had committed the murder. The part of Ranger in *The Suspicious Husband* was one of Garrick's favourites and Sarah was terrified that she would let him down. She got through it well enough, although the papers did not mention her performance at all, for Garrick to inform her that she was to play Lady Anne opposite his Richard III in Shakespeare's play.

When she heard this Sarah's spirits did rise because this really was an honour. In a few days' time Garrick, the incomparable Garrick, was retiring from the stage for ever and obviously he could have had any actress he wanted to play Lady Anne. No one could imagine what the theatre, and Drury Lane in particular, would be like without him; to actors and playgoers alike he was something quite apart. It was hard, too, to imagine how he would get on without the theatre – what he would do with himself. It was not as if he were old, he was only fifty-nine. The Siddonses realized that Sarah's own position at Drury Lane would be more precarious when he was no longer manager, so they welcomed this chance particularly.

Garrick rehearsed her hard for it. Though he was patient he was also exacting in rehearsals. Kitty Clive, an actress who played with him often described him at rehearsals 'with lamb-like patience *endeavouring* to beat his ideas into the heads of creatures who have none of their own.' He always knew what he wanted and was prepared to take a lot of trouble to get it. He once told another young actor, 'If you cannot give a speech or make love to a table, chair, or marble, as well as to the finest woman in the world, you are not, nor ever will be, a great actor.' He meant by this that the emotion, the intelligence, the *character* must be within the player, so that he *is* the part he is playing, no matter what the circumstances around him might be.

Sarah admitted that she learned a lot from seeing him act and from watching him take a rehearsal, but she did not like his criticisms. He found fault with the way she held her arms. Flustered and worried she tried to do what he told her, although she did not agree with him. Looking back, she came to believe that he criticized her because he could not bear her 'to shade the tip of his nose' as she put it, or in other words, steal the limelight from him, but this is obviously nonsense. Garrick was much too well established to be jealous of anyone, certainly not a nervous beginner, and anyway, even if he thought Sarah would become a great actress she could not be a rival to him because he was about to retire.

One of the things that Garrick was always very determined upon was that the audience should see his face. He believed, with reason, that he was the person they had particularly come to see and that the rest of the cast, though they had to act well, were there as supports for him. He insisted therefore, that when he was speaking to other players they must have their backs to the audience and be downstage from him, so that his face was always clearly visible to the whole auditorium. On the whole, audiences for many years before his time and for many years after, went to the theatre to see a particular player in a particular part. They did not expect, and probably would not have wanted as we do now, to see plays presented by a team of actors, with every character, however small, being as nearly perfect as possible, so that the thing that matters is the play as a whole and not just one brilliant performance.

To her horror, on the first night she played Lady Anne, Sarah forgot this rule of Garrick's. It was really his fault because in the scene in which Richard sees the ghost he was so natural that she completely forgot everything but the play. She did not move away as she should have done and in order to look at her, he had to look away from the audience at one of his most tremendous moments. He gave her a glare she never forgot as long as she lived. It upset her so much that she did not know how she got through the rest of the scene and she trembled to think what he would say to her. To her relief he said nothing. No doubt he put the lapse down to first-night nerves and was sure she would never do it again, as indeed she never did.

Five nights later the Drury Lane season came to an end and David Garrick retired.

Of course Sarah was not satisfied with her part in this season. All her dreams of taking London by storm had died away. She had not had a single good notice, not even for Lady Anne. That year's May edition of *The London Magazine*, after praising Garrick said: 'As to most of the other characters, particularly the female ones, they were wretchedly performed. Mrs Hopkins was an ungracious Queen, Mrs Johnson a frightful Duchess and Mrs Siddons a lamentable Lady Anne.' This no one could call encouraging, even allowing for the fact that at such a moment all the praise would tend to be lavished on Garrick himself.

But although Sarah had not enjoyed her first Drury Lane season because she had not acted well and was neither tough nor belligerent enough to hold her own against hostile and jealous players, she had not wasted her time. She had learned a lot from Garrick, even though she did not like being told, and even more from watching him take rehearsals and from seeing him and the other players at work. She had gained, too, from acting on a big stage, with experienced people and before more educated audiences. One thing she had not learned, and did not mean to, was to be temperamental and to make trouble behind the scenes and at rehearsals. For those who had not been present, it was hard to believe anyone could behave as Mrs Yates and Miss Younge did, yelling and screaming, quarrelling, flying into ungovernable rages, sulking, holding up rehearsals and generally making themselves an intolerable nuisance to everyone. Sarah liked to come on to the stage for rehearsals and get down to work on the play in hand at once, accommodating herself to the other actors and hoping they would do the same to her. She never, even at the height of her fame made unnecessary trouble. She despised such behaviour.

Neither Sarah nor William considered taking a holiday when the Drury Lane season was over. Living in London was expensive and lodging-house landladies had to be paid every week. There was no difficulty about getting work for Sarah, and Richard Yates signed her up at once to play in the western counties again. He was delighted to have an actress straight from Drury Lane. It looked very well on the posters.

They thought the engagement with Yates would only be for the summer; they did not doubt that Sarah, at any rate, would be back again at Drury Lane next season. William did write to Garrick asking him to recommend them to the new managers, Sheridan, Linley and Forde, but this was merely a precaution because all contracts lapsed when a new management took over. The new contract would just be a formality because they confidently expected that Sarah would be re-engaged on the old terms.

The blow fell when they were in Birmingham. William had a letter from W. Hopkins, the prompter at Drury Lane, written for Sheridan and Company, simply saying they were not proposing to renew the Siddonses contract.

Sarah was staggered. At first she simply could not believe it, and when she did she became so depressed that it made her ill. Years later she wrote, 'It was a stunning and cruel blow, overwhelming all my ambitious hopes and involving peril even to the subsistence of my helpless babes. It was very near destroying me. My blighted prospects, indeed, induced a state of mind that preyed upon my health and for a year and a half I was supposed to be hastening to a decline.'

It was a wretched time. She felt very ill from nervous depression, she seriously doubted her own powers as an actress, and if she could not make a success on the stage the future looked grim. William certainly could not support them by his acting and there did not seem anything else he could do. Their whole existence depended on Sarah so however disheartened she felt, she had to go on acting. For some time she was sick of everything connected with the theatre, but she accepted every offer that came her way, thankful to have the money even though she often felt so ill that she wondered if she could get through her part.

No one at Drury Lane regretted her going, though Mrs Abington, who had never been quite so vindictive as the others, did say she thought Sheridan was a fool to let such an actress go.

As the months passed Sarah began to feel better. Several things helped her to get back to her old self. To begin with her prestige as an actress who had played with Garrick at Drury Lane meant that she had very different treatment now from that in the old touring days. She was not now asked to play in dusty barns and inn yards, setting up sometimes just for a night and then moving on, but was engaged to play in the few good theatres in the more enlightened county towns and to give a number of performances in each. There was no more turning up in a town and hoping to find somewhere to play. Now her arrival was billed weeks beforehand. Also she was nearly always given the big parts, to interpret as she liked, and this was just what she needed to build up her morale. And even though she did not in the least want to copy the tantrums, the hysterics and the downright rudeness of Mrs Yates and Miss Younge, it was soothing to her pride to be considered the most important person in her scenes.

To theatre managers such a leading actress was a joy. Someone who did not make endless fusses and demand the best of everything for herself, nor go round making trouble with the cast and back-stage people was rare enough to be very welcome. She was some-times accused of being aloof and over-dignified because no one realized that this came simply from shyness, but even then she was always polite and kind to the other actors and the dressers and stage-hands.

Up to this time in her life Sarah was simply what theatrical people call 'a natural', by which they mean a person who speaks and moves well, can express emotion, has good timing, and a strong sense of drama. Sarah had all these things in abundance, and beside that was unusually beautiful, graceful and intelligent. She also had an inborn power to thrill and move an audience, but up to now had never really made an effort to become the person she was playing, to get right inside the character until she was one with it. She began to get an idea of doing this when she was between twenty and twenty-one years old, while she was touring for Yates.

It happened because she was to play Lady Macbeth the next day for the first time. For some reason they had had no rehearsals, prob-ably because the manager had changed his mind about what they were to play, and Sarah had not even studied the part. It seems extraordinary to us that any company could think of putting on a play without rehearsing it first, but the situation was different then. In a play as well known as Macbeth all, or almost all the players, would have acted in it before and would know their parts. To a large extent all the action and business would be the same wherever and with whoever it was played, and for this reason rehearsals were always fewer than would be needed nowadays. It was unusual to have no rehearsal at all, but Sarah was quite sure that provided she knew what Lady Macbeth said and did she would get through per-fectly well.

As usual she waited until everyone else had gone to bed and then settled down to study. She was so quick at learning words that she was sure she would know them by the morning. She was familiar with the play of course, and had seen it acted a number of times, but she had never given any real thought before to Lady Macbeth as a person. Now she did, and as she read on by the light of one candle, in the silent house, the scenes became more and more real to her until the horror of the murder was too vivid and she simply could not go on. She snatched up her candle and ran out of the room in a panic. As she hurried up the stairs the rustling of her silk dress seemed to be some awful ghostly creature coming after her and she fled the faster. She ran into her bedroom where William was asleep and, too frightened either to put out the candle or to get undressed, she simply flung herself into bed and lay there palpitating with terror, the horror of what Lady Macbeth did all about her.

In the morning she felt calmer and rather ashamed of her panic, but as she thought about it she realized that for the first time in her life she had become so lost in a character that the situation she was in was absolutely real to her. She found that she understood something of Lady Macbeth and how she felt and she realized what exciting possibilities it opened up. She was thrilled by this idea and from now on determined to study every part she played in this way.

But though an experience like this, and the use she put it to, made her such a wonderful actress in the future, it certainly did not make for a good performance of Lady Macbeth that first time. She had not learnt the words well and had to have a phenomenal number of prompts. She was never quite sure what she ought to be doing and she gave an appalling performance which so mortified and embarrassed her that she made herself promise that she would never go on a stage again without proper rehearsals.

Sarah soon found that this new way of study made every part far more interesting and improved her acting enormously. It was soon obvious, too, the increasing impact it was making on audiences. In Birmingham, York, Liverpool and Manchester her reputation began to grow and grow. One of the actors who played opposite her, Mr Henderson (said by some people to be the greatest Shylock and Iago ever seen) was tremendously impressed with her. He advised Mr Palmer, the manager of the Theatre Royal, Bath to add her to his company as soon as he possibly could – she was unique, he said, no other young actress like her had ever been seen. Palmer explained that he could not ask her for that season, he had actresses enough, but he determined to do so for the next, and hoped no one would sign her up in the meantime.

Sarah was never out of a job and acted all the great parts of the day. She even appeared as Hamlet again – she was so slender she could play a man fairly convincingly – and she gave a brilliant interpretation. As time went on and the bitterness of her mortification about Drury Lane faded she found she was enjoying herself. It was still an exacting life she was leading. Moving from place to place so often with two small children was not easy, even though William took over all the arrangements and of course they had a nurse, but it was stimulating and fun. And this new way of approaching her parts had made her like acting again.

She and William made two very good new friends too, the Inchbalds, who were also actors. Elizabeth Inchbald, who wrote plays as well, was particularly charming and gay and Sarah loved her. She was pretty and intelligent with a very slight stammer. Another pleasant thing was that John joined them. He had been happy at Douai, but the pull of the theatre was too strong and he gave up all idea of becoming a priest and came back to England to become an actor. Of course he went at once to Sarah; she was the most likely person to help him to get a start on the stage, and later, in the spring of 1777 he and the Siddonses – babies and all – and the Inchbalds all took a holiday together. They went to a farm at Russell Moor, near Appledurcombe and it was the first real country holiday Sarah had ever had. She enjoyed herself so much, just being with her family and with leisure to give them, even washing, ironing and sewing for them, that she went about all day singing and talking nonsense with John and the Inchbalds. She had time to go for walks on the moor and play blind-man's-buff and puss in the corner with the children, who were now four and two years old. In the evening the grown-ups played cards or listened to John and Sarah singing duets.

The holiday did Sarah good, but she still looked delicate and when she was engaged to play at York just afterwards she seemed so fragile to the manager, Tate Wilkinson, that he wondered if she would be strong enough to play her exacting parts. People were always wondering this, she looked so willowy and delicate, but actually Sarah was quite strong; she could never have led such a strenuous life if she had not been.

7 Theatre Royal, Bath

It was in October the following year that Mr Palmer engaged her to play at Bath. Sarah was very pleased to go. For one thing it meant much less travelling, the family could settle in Bath. Then, that town had the best theatre and the most intelligent audiences outside London. It was a delightful place to live in, too, and claimed, with reason, to be the most cultured and fashionable city in England after London.

Sarah knew Mr Henderson had recommended her warmly (he had said, in fact, that she was an actress 'who never had an equal nor would ever have a superior') so she was surprised and rather annoyed to find, when she joined the theatre, that the Thursday nights when she was to play the leading parts were the night on which the Cotillion Balls were held at the Assembly Rooms. These balls were among the most fashionable entertainments in Bath, and all the *élite* went to them. In a town like Bath, which had its regular theatre company engaged for the season, each well-known player expected to play the leading parts on one night in each week. Palmer explained eagerly that he could not ask his other leading actresses to change their nights or he would not have asked her to play on the one night of the week when there was a strong counter-attraction. He was pleasantly surprised when Sarah took this news calmly and without a scene even though she was not pleased. He did not know another leading actress who would have done so.

On the first two Thursdays Mr Palmer put on comedies and for some time past now Sarah had felt that she was better in tragedy and that comic parts were not really her line. Certainly no one took much notice of her début in Bath, but on the third Thursday she played Elwina in a tragedy called *Percy* by Hannah More, and the Bath critics set up. According to the *Bath Chronicle* next morning: 'Mrs Siddons was established in the judgement of the town as the most capital actress that has performed here these many years.'

And people continued to talk. So much so that more and more of them stopped going to the Cotillion Balls and went to the Theatre Royal in Orchard Street instead, to see young Mrs Siddons act.

In spite of this success Sarah did not get star treatment. She had been engaged at a salary of £3 a week, less than London but quite usual for the provinces, and she certainly earned it. She started each Monday with a rehearsal at the Bath Theatre, and then hurried away by coach to play that night at Bristol, where Palmer had another theatre, a journey of about thirteen miles which would have taken two to three hours. On Tuesday she came back to Bath in time to play there that night. On Wednesday she might have to go back to Bristol and Thursday, of course, was her important night when she was sure of playing the lead in Bath. On Friday she was at Bristol again and on Saturday she came back to Bath. It depended, of course, on the plays whether she was acting every night, but by the terms of her contract she had to play smaller parts whenever she was wanted, and she was wanted a great deal – by Mr Palmer if not by the other actors. Audiences had a tendency to notice Mrs Siddons, however small her part, more than they noticed the leading players, especially if she had to be sad or pathetic. She could move people to tears more easily than anyone.

The Siddonses stayed four years in Bath, from 1778 to 1782 and they loved it there. Life was full and gay and rewarding even if for Sarah the work was hard. They made many friends and had two more babies, Maria, born on 1 July 1779, and Frances Amelia, born in 1781 who only lived a month or two.

Bath was not only fashionable, it was full of intelligent and cultured people and Sarah and William made most of their friends among these. They were particularly fond of the Rev. Thomas Whalley and his wife, Mrs Thrale and Miss Western, and they were also friendly with Hannah More and Anna Seward. Although Mr Whalley had a living in Lincolnshire he lived in Bath because the bishop who presented him to the living had made him promise not to live there as he was sure the climate would not suit him. Mr Whalley accordingly put in a curate to do the duty (presumably a man acclimatized to the noxious Lincoln air!), married a rich wife, and settled in Bath. He was tall, thin, handsome and sentimental, and aspired to be a patron of the arts. He was also a very loyal friend. He loved and admired Sarah all his life, and she loved him and Mrs Whalley in return. Mrs Thrale was a lively, talkative, slightly malicious but basically kind woman, with two daughters about the same ages as the Siddonses little girls. She was the sort of person who always knows everything about her friends, not always accurately, and sometimes a good deal more than they know themselves. She was a great letter writer and one of her correspondents was Dr Samuel Johnson.

Almost anyone who was anyone came to Bath; various members of the large Royal Family, the brilliant and beautiful Duchess of Devonshire (she often came – Gainsborough painted her famous portrait while she was staying in Bath) and Fanny Burney who had just written *Evelina*. Samuel Johnson stayed there occasionally and once, a little lame boy whose name was Walter Scott was brought to Bath to drink the waters for his health.

Sarah also met Thomas Lawrence again. He was twelve now, still as handsome as ever and even more interesting because, child though he was, he had set up as a fashionable portrait painter with his own studio, in order to contribute towards his family's expenses. He had a number of brothers and sisters now and his father was as hopeless as ever at keeping a job, so if it had not been for Thomas they would have been in difficulties. He adored Sarah, partly because she was so beautiful and partly because she was an actress; at one time he had thought of going on the stage and he was always fascinated by the theatre. He painted at least one portrait of Sarah while she was in Bath.

Among the people who went to see her act was old Mr Sheridan, father of Richard Brinsley Sheridan, author of *The Rivals* and now part manager of Drury Lane. Sheridan senior had seen Sarah in *The Runaway* in London and had not thought much of her. In fact he had been surprised to hear Garrick say that he thought 'she possessed enough powers to delight and electrify an audience'; it was not the impression he had at all. However, when all Bath was talking so much about this brilliant young actress he felt perhaps he ought to go and see her again. He chose an unfortunate evening because, through some muddle, the costume she was supposed to wear had not arrived from Bristol and she had to appear in her ordinary clothes. But Mr Sheridan was astounded. He wrote to his son immediately, 'No disadvantage of dress could conceal her transcendental merit.'

He was so impressed that he rushed round to her dressing-room after the play to congratulate her and give her advice. He believed she was wasted in Bath, good as her audiences were, and when he returned to London he did his best to persuade his son to engage her. In spite of the memory she had left in Drury Lane, Richard Sheridan had enough confidence in his father to agree to make an effort to get her. Also he had Sarah recommended very strongly to him by Mr Henderson.

It was a tremendous triumph for Sarah – to have Drury Lane asking her to go back. But though she was thrilled to be asked, she did not want to go. Her memories were unpleasant and she was more than contented where she was. She liked Bath as a town much better than London and also her sister Fanny had just joined the company and she wanted to be there to help her. She turned the offer down.

But old Mr Sheridan would not give up. He kept on begging his son to engage her and Richard Brinsley kept on trying, and in the following year, 1782, he was successful. He offered Sarah £10 a week and two benefits a season, and she and William felt it was too good an offer to be refused. They were expecting their fifth child (another girl, Elizabeth Anne was born on 2nd June) and with four children to support they felt it would be wrong for them to turn such a good opportunity down.

Sarah hated having to take such a decision. She really did not like London, and she was nervous about going back. It meant exchanging certainty for risk. She was known and loved in Bath and was certain of good audiences whenever she acted and therefore of a steady salary. She could not be sure she would be any more successful in London this time than she had been before. If Palmer had realized earlier what was happening and had offered a rise in salary, she would have stayed with him, but he left it too late and did nothing until she had signed up with Drury Lane.

Not only Palmer but the whole of Bath was bitterly disappointed when they heard she was going. So much so that Sarah, who always took audiences seriously, decided she had better say something about it. She chose her usual way of doing this, the recitation of a poem (the combined work once more of William and herself) at the end of her last performance on May 21st. All the posters stated that Mrs Siddons would give her 'serious reasons for her departure' as an Epilogue.

Accordingly, when the final curtain had come down on *The Distressed Mother*, it rose again as Sarah advanced to the footlights, and when the applause had died down, began to recite her poem. After the opening lines which were so banal that it looks as if William composed them on his own, she went on :

'Why don't I here, you'll say, content remain,
Nor seek uncertainties for certain gain?

'To argue here would but your time abuse :
I keep my word, my reason I produce.'

With her sure sense of the dramatic Sarah then swept to the wings where Henry, now eight, Sally, six and a half, and Maria, not quite three, were waiting. They were all good-looking children and not at all shy. Taking Maria in her arms, Sally by the hand and with Henry walking beside her, Sarah returned to the footlights to say :

'These are the moles that bear me from your side,
Where I was rooted, where I could have died.

'Have I been hasty? Am I then to blame?
Answer all ye who bear a parent's name . . .'

She looked so beautiful and stately, and made such a charming picture of a young mother with her three delightful children that the audience, pardoning the bad poetry, roared and yelled, clapped and stamped until she swept a magnificent curtsy and retired, the applause thundering on and on as she did so.

8　Drury Lane Again

Although Elizabeth Anne had only been born early in June, and although her farewell benefit brought her in £393, Sarah was acting again throughout July. The move to London was bound to be expensive and she did not feel she ought to turn down any engagement, so she went back to Bristol. William took the children to Weymouth for a holiday by the sea and Sarah allowed herself to join them in August. She had a very long journey from Bristol to Weymouth and wrote a description of it to the Whalleys.

There were four people besides Sarah inside the coach and as she turned her large, dark eyes from one to another she decided that one of the ladies was 'a little insane'. 'Her dress,' she wrote, 'was the most peculiar, and manner the most offensive, I ever remember to have met with; her person was taller and more thin than you can imagine; her hair raven black, drawn as tight as possible over her cushion before and behind; and at the top of her head was placed a solitary flycap of the last century, composed of materials of about twenty sorts and as dirty as the ground; her neck, which was a thin scrap of a quarter of a yard long, and the colour of a walnut, she wore uncovered, for the solace of all beholders; her Circassian was an olive-coloured cotton of three several sorts, about two breadths wide in the skirt, and tied up exactly in the middle in one place only. She had a black petticoat spotted with red, and over that a very thin white muslin one, with a long black gauze apron, and without the least hoop.' It hardly seems possible that anyone could go about in clothes as odd as these, but this unfortunate woman's behaviour was even odder than her appearance. She flew into a 'violent passion' when she noticed one of the windows was open, and when Sarah, anxious to be pleasant, had put it up for her 'she began to scold the woman who sat opposite to her for touching her foot'. Nothing suited her, and when Sarah, still trying to be nice to her offered to make tea for her at breakfast (they had left Bristol very early in the morning) she found she did no good. 'Vain,' she wrote, 'were my endeavours to please this strange creature. She desired to have her tea in a basin, and I followed her directions as near as it was possible in the making of her tea; but she no sooner tasted it than she bounced to the window and threw it out, declaring she had never met with such a set of awkward, ill-bred people.' This mad woman then snatched the canister of tea from Sarah, poured a quantity of tea into the basin, added sugar, cream and water together and drank it all off.

All the coach passengers did their best to calm this extraordinary creature. One woman, Sarah said, was more successful at dealing with her and kept her under some sort of control. Unfortunately the mad woman went all the way to Weymouth with them and 'the journey was made almost intolerable by her fretfulness'. She kept on getting in a panic that the coach would upset, or that the guard had lost her luggage, and though it was stiflingly hot, refused to have any windows open. They were all thankful to arrive, and Sarah was delighted to find William waiting for her. In spite of the tediousness of her journey she was in good spirits, very pleased to be with her family and even 'a deplorable lodging' where the 'water and bread are intolerable' did not upset her. 'Travellers must be content,' she wrote philosophically.

The whole family went up to London at the end of September to their new lodgings at 149 The Strand. Drury Lane posters had already announced that 'Mrs Siddons (from the Theatre Royal, Bath) will shortly make her appearance in a capital Character in Tragedy', but the name of the play had not been given because it had not yet been decided. Sarah wanted it to be *The Grecian Daughter* but she was persuaded by the Sheridans to make her first appearance as Isabella in *The Fatal Marriage* when her powers of moving audiences to tears would be given full play. Old Thomas Sheridan, who had become very fond of her, advised his son to have her opening night as soon as possible. He knew the state of nerves she was in. It was arranged for 10 October, and for even that short time Sarah found the waiting almost more than she could bear. 'For a whole fortnight before this (to me) memorable day,' she wrote, 'I suffered from nervous agitation more than can be imagined. No wonder! For my own fate and that of my little family, hung upon it. I had quitted Bath, where all my efforts had been successful, and I feared lest a second failure in London might influence the public mind greatly to my prejudice, in the event of my return from Drury Lane, disgraced as I formerly had been.'

Although she had played Isabella many times before, she gave as much thought to it now as if she had never seen the part. She had always been impatient of the stage convention that all the actions were to be the same every time the play was acted, no matter who acted it, and was always ready to try out new moves, new inflections, even entirely new interpretations.

When she got down to the theatre for the first rehearsal of Isabella she was in a panic. One of her fears was that she would not be heard. Last time she had played in Drury Lane she was nearly inaudible and even in Bath some critics had said she was not always easy to hear. This morning she asked old Mr Sheridan to go to the very back of the theatre to listen. He had taken to coming to the theatre when she was rehearsing and she liked him to. He would sit watching her as she re-created in words and actions the character she had already created in her mind from her study of the part when she was alone, and she found his comments and advice were often helpful. To her immense relief, when she got over her nervousness and spoke out she could be heard perfectly from all over the house.

As usual, as the rehearsal went on she forgot everything but Isabella – she *was* Isabella. She almost forgot she was in the theatre and she certainly gave no thought to what other people were thinking of her performance until she realized that a number of the other players were openly crying, although their parts called for no tears. Her playing was so true and so moving they could not help it.

This encouraged her and the second rehearsal went even better. She was so realistic and so pathetic, especially in the scene when Isabella dies, that Henry Siddons (although he was only eight he was playing Isabella's son) was completely overcome and roared and cried, believing that his mother really was dying. Sarah had hastily to come to life again and hug him before he was reassured.

At the end of this second rehearsal she left the theatre feeling confident she would not disgrace herself on the great night, and she continued to feel perfectly happy until later that evening when she suddenly thought she was losing her voice and that, when she did get it back, it sounded hoarse. It was nothing but nerves, but of course she imagined all sorts of things were wrong and, above all, dreaded that the opening night would have to be put off. However a night's sleep and the fact that the sun was shining next day, which she took to be a happy omen, brought her voice back to normal and the panic was over.

The whole Kemble family were waiting breathlessly to see how Sarah was received by London audiences. Her father could not stay away, but came to London to be with her on her great night. When the moment came for them to set off for the theatre he alone went with her, because William was in such a state of nerves that they all realized that, far from being any support to her, he would only upset her.

Now that the moment had come, in spite of the good rehearsals when they got to the theatre Sarah was in the state she called 'one of my desperate tranquillities'. She went down to her dressing-room in the basement of the theatre where her dressers were waiting and never spoke one word all the time she was getting ready. She sighed heavily once or twice but she simply could not speak. She saw the women look at each other, wondering if she were all right because she was usually friendly and talkative, but she said afterwards she could not have said a word to them.

At last she heard herself called to what she expressed as 'her fiery trial'. The moment had come. She walked out of her dressing-room and climbed the stairs to the stage.

She never forgot what she felt at that moment as long as she lived. She described it as 'the awful consciousness that one is the sole object of attention to that immense space, lined as it were with human intellect from top to bottom and all around'. With this 'awful consciousness' on her she heard her cue, took Henry's hand, took in a deep breath and walked on.

Theatrical history was made that evening. Sarah's impact on the audience was only equalled by Garrick's first performance as Richard III when he had astounded playgoers forty years before. The audience was so thrilled and moved to pity that they were completely overcome and nearly everyone was crying. Many women had hysterics and one or two fainted. James Boarden, who afterwards wrote a biography of Sarah and who was in the theatre that night, said that at first 'literally the greater part of the spectators were too ill to use their hands in applause'. No one had ever seen such an Isabella. Sarah did not rant and rave, nor stand speaking blank verse in an emotional way, she just was the unhappy woman who, in spite of being innocent, in spite of her tenderness and faithfulness was forced by the harshness of her father-in-law into bigamy, madness and suicide. After her death the applause was so tremendous and prolonged that for a long time the scene could not be finished. When Sarah wrote to the Whalleys to tell them about this triumphant evening she said, 'As I know it will give you pleasure I venture to assure you I never in my life heard such peals of applause. I thought they would not have suffered Mr Packer to end the play. Oh! how I wished for you last night to share a joy which was too much for me to bear alone! My poor husband was so agitated he durst not venture near the house.'

When it was all over and she could get away she and Mr Kemble went home to tell the agitated William what had happened. They were all too exhausted emotionally to celebrate and just sat down to an ordinary supper. Sarah was too excited and overjoyed to speak, but William occasionally broke the silence with 'exclamations of gladness'. Every now and then Mr Kemble would put down his knife and fork and look at Sarah, while tears of joy which he did not even bother to wipe away rolled down his face. All three were thinking of the years of struggle and hard work on cold, draughty stages, acting to boorish yokels – those years that began when a little girl recited 'The Fable of the Boys and the Frogs' and led to this evening of superlative triumph.

They did not sit up after supper, they were all too worn out, but tired as she was it was over an hour before Sarah fell asleep – she was remembering so many things.

She did not wake till the middle of the next day and then, of course, her first interest was to see her notices in the papers. Every paper was full of praise, and nothing but praise. The *Morning Post* put her above the great Mrs Cibber and said that 'she was beyond all comparison the first tragic actress now on the English stage'. As Mrs Cibber's reputation had become almost legendary this was high praise indeed and made all the more exciting when she and William and Mr Kemble compared it with the frightful notices she had had when she played in London before.

Everybody wanted to see this wonderful young actress as Isabella, and the play was repeated eight times in twenty days. She thought her performance improved as she went on, and audiences certainly agreed with her. The whole town was talking about her and it became a 'must' for everyone to go and see young Mrs Siddons. It was all tremendously exciting, though William and Sarah agreed they must keep their heads. This was quite hard to do especially when a body as august as the Law Society gave her a hundred guineas for 'her wonderful playing'. This was unexpected and pleasing enough, but it was followed by something even more gratifying, at least to Sarah. The management of Drury Lane changed her dressing-room from the inconvenient basement one she was first given, to the one that had been Mr Garrick's. It was not only that his room was much larger and better furnished and on a level with and near to the stage, it was the thrill of being thought worthy of his dressing-room that pleased Sarah. 'Oh unexpected happiness!' she exclaimed. 'It is impossible to conceive my gratification when I saw my own figure in the self-same glass which had so often reflected the face and form of that unequalled genius – not perhaps without some vague, fanciful hope of a little degree of inspiration from it.'

There was much discussion as to what her next play should be. The Sheridans agreed at last that it should be, as Sarah wanted, *The Grecian Daughter*, to be played on 30 October. The part of Euphrasia, dignified, tragic and in places wildly heroic was completely different from that of Isabella. As soon as the play was announced everyone was agog to see what Mrs Siddons made of it. She made an instant success, but was so different from Isabella that those who had seen her in her first play could hardly believe they were looking at the same woman. Not only was her personality changed, but her appearance and build. Sarah looked taller as Euphrasia than she had as Isabella, and not only taller, but larger and with a more powerful physique.

An agitating thing happened one night when she was playing Euphrasia that could have ended in real tragedy. In one scene she had to stab Dionysius, who was played by an actor called John Palmer, and as usual had a stage dagger, the blade of which slid up the hilt when it was pressed against anything. To Palmer's pain and Sarah's horror on this occasion the blade did not retract when she struck him and she really drove it into him. Luckily his costume was made of thick material, and luckily too, she struck him so far to the side that the dagger only grazed his ribs, but Sarah was horrified to see real blood seeping out of his wound as he lay on the stage. As she could have killed him it was no wonder both he and she were agitated. Strangely enough John Palmer did die on the stage some years later, though not through being stabbed.

In November Sarah played Jane Shore. She had come a long way from the time she acted the part to Garrick as a girl of seventeen.

Now she could understand Jane and play her as she should be played. London audiences were beginning to expect marvels from Sarah, but it was a mystery how a young and beautiful woman could make herself into a starving, emaciated skeleton, with hollowed, glittering eyes that finally glazed in death. It was one of the wonderful things about Sarah that she could do this; make-up was not so well understood then, nor so skilfully applied, but somehow she managed it. A Miss Wynn who saw her as Jane Shore said, 'Mrs Siddons ceased to excite pleasure by her appearance, I absolutely thought her the creature perishing through want, "fainting from loss of food"; shocked at the sight I could not avoid turning from the suffering object.'

London playgoers were packing the theatre on the nights Sarah played, and brawls and commotions took place every night. Although most of the seats were booked beforehand, late-comers and the people who, hearing she was acting decided to see her, kept arriving, pushing and shoving at the pit door, which in Drury Lane was near the stage. Added to those coming in were the ladies being carried out, overcome with emotion because of her acting, and free-for-all fights took place quite often. The noise and commotion was alarming and distracting to the actors, but Sarah had to get used to it, it happened so often.

She had her first benefit on 14 December, and after much discussion with the Sheridans and William, chose *Venice Preserved*, perhaps because it had brought her luck when Lord Bruce and Miss Boyle had seen it in Cheltenham seven years ago, but also, no doubt, because Belvidera was always one of her favourite parts. It is a difficult one, as Belvidera experiences one violent emotion after another so quickly, but it gave her such scope that she loved it.

There was an enormous demand for seats. Usually at a benefit the management kept six boxes for themselves, but on this occasion they agreed they ought to make some acknowledgement of the money Sarah was making for them, so they included their boxes in her takings for the night. Sarah was gratified, but knew it was no more than her due. She was packing the theatre for them as no other player could and they were only paying her £10 a week, not a great salary. She and William were glad of the extra money because London was a much more expensive place to live in than Bath.

9 Success

Sarah's popularity was something quite out of the ordinary; no other player of her time came anywhere near it. Everyone was talking about her and whenever she appeared in the streets she was mobbed. Being a shy, reserved person this was rather overwhelming and her instinctive reaction was to become, in public, more reserved and dignified than ever. Naturally this made many people think her proud but in fact this was undeserved; all the adulation she received did not make her conceited or arrogant.

She never courted publicity. As soon as a play was over she preferred to go home to William and the children, and much as she adored applause in the theatre, outside it she wished people would leave her alone. She did not make many close friends, but she kept in constant touch with the people she loved.

She was also ready to go to any trouble to help any member of her family to the stage careers they all longed for. John did not need her help; he was making a name for himself in Dublin – so much so that the Drury Lane management were trying to get him to join them for the next season – but she helped Fanny and Elizabeth by persuading Richard Sheridan to give them a trial in Drury Lane.

The Kembles remained very much alike even after they grew up and Fanny and Elizabeth were pretty girls, but as it turned out their likeness to Sarah was more of a handicap than an asset. They were not as beautiful and audiences were not interested in a not-so-pretty repeat of their favourite, who was not a good actress either. There was a great deal of excitement on the first night that Fanny, now just twenty-four, was to appear with Sarah – London playgoers were keen to see if she would be another genius. The crowd at the theatre was so great that thousands had to be turned away and those who did get in were squeezed and shoved, stamped on and even lamed, and nearly all had their pockets picked. Grand ladies, when they finally got to their seats, found their dresses ruined, with hoops pushed out of shape and lace and flounces torn off. It was a deplorable start for any performance and if Fanny had been another genius she could hardly have put the spectators in a good mood after such experiences. The play was *Jane Shore* again, and Fanny played Alicia, the other big woman's part, who was a horrible and wicked person, but much livelier than Jane. Fanny, who was nervous, inexperienced and completely overshadowed by Sarah, was hopeless, and the public and Press were not slow in saying so. Sarah, though disappointed was undaunted. She, too, had had bad notices at first. She refused to accept the fact that the sisters were not good actresses and she made Sheridan give both Fanny and Elizabeth parts throughout the rest of the season. But all her pushing was no good; neither of made any success in London.

Of course being so successful meant that Sarah made a lot more money. Her second benefit – she played Zara in Congreve's *Mourning Bride* – brought in even more than her first. William occasionally took tiny parts, but he made practically no money himself, he just managed Sarah's. All her earnings went to him and he simply gave her back spending money (about a tenth of what she earned) for her clothes both on and off the stage. The rest was treated as family income, naturally, as she was the bread-winner. What does seem odd now was that all this money, though entirely earned by Sarah, was legally William's. But before the Married Woman's Property Act in 1882 a married woman could not own any money. She could not touch a penny without her husband's permission.

Because this was normal Sarah did not object to it at all, and anyway she and William did not quarrel or argue about how it ought to be spent, or how much Sarah should have for herself. They neither of them wanted to be lavish, but they did decide that they could afford a carriage, which would be useful in getting to the theatre and back. Hackney coaches were usually dirty and often hard to get, and when Sarah walked she was mobbed. It would also be useful for returning some of the calls that all the grand Londoners had begun to make on her. There was very often a traffic jam outside No. 149 Strand, coaches, phaetons and chaises blocking the way for hours.

Sarah was much too shy to enjoy large parties and seldom went to them. Besides, she had neither the time nor energy for them. Acting took a lot out of her, and what with rehearsing, studying her parts, performing, and managing her home and children she had as full a life as she could manage. When she went out at all, she enjoyed small dinner-parties with friends, though even then she had some experiences that made her chary of accepting any invitations unless she knew the people really well.

On one occasion she was asked to a party by a Miss Moncton. Sarah was not much drawn to her – she was a strange, squat-looking woman who was supposed to be a blue-stocking and who added to her already queer appearance by wearing extraordinary clothes, a lot of diamonds, too much rouge and towering headdresses – but she agreed to go. The party was on a Sunday evening and, thinking it was to be a small affair, Sarah arrived at about eight o'clock, simply dressed. Henry had been asked too, more for 'effect than his *beaux yeux*', Sarah surmised, which was why she had arrived so early. Parties usually started between ten and eleven, but she meant to get back in good time. She enjoyed herself more than she expected, and so stayed longer.

She was just getting up to go when there were thunderous knocks on the front door and literally masses of people poured in. 'Such a throng,' she said, she had 'never before encountered in any private house.' The crowd was so great she could not push her way through to get out, and then, to her mortification and annoyance, she realized that they had simply come to look at her. They shoved each other (and her) to get near and some even climbed on chairs to stare at her and, worse still, she was set upon by a group of earnest, high-brow women, nicknamed *The Blues*, who asked her what she thought a lot of ridiculous questions. Her honesty and good sense prevented her from trying to pretend she knew the answers when she did not, so she simply said she knew very little of what they were talking about, but she thought them stupid and tiresome in the extreme. One man had the bad manners to discuss her acting in front of her without bringing her into the conversation at all, and this sort of thing went on till the small hours of the morning. Sarah controlled herself very well in spite of her annoyance, and Fanny Burney, who was also there, said that she 'behaved with great propriety and was calm, modest and unaffected'. She did also think she was 'stiff and un-bending'; no doubt disgust made Sarah at her most aloof. Her final embarrassment came when a 'young muse' – a girl in a white frock with a fillet of flowers tied round her hair, which hung down her back in flowing curls' was presented to her with great ceremony. Sarah did not know what she was supposed to do and was blushing and embarrassed. The girl, who was thoroughly enjoying being able to show off in front of the great Mrs Siddons, was quite at her ease, and recited a poem which began :

'O thou, whom Nature's goodness calls her own
Pride of the stage and favourite of the town.'

Sarah went home in a rage. She considered the whole evening an example of grossly bad manners and resented being treated as if she were a circus spectacle to be stared at. There was nothing she loathed more, off the stage, than being treated as an exhibition.

She had other experiences of people's effrontery. She was sitting in her drawing-room one morning, having given orders that she was not to be disturbed when her maid burst in saying that there were some ladies below who insisted on seeing her, although they had been told she was particularly engaged and could see no one, and who, even at that minute, were coming up the stairs.

Sarah, to her amazement, did hear footsteps, and before she could do anything about it the maid was pushed to one side and a procession of five women came slowly in. She did not know any of them. The leading one was tall and elegant, but looked ill. Looking the personification of outraged dignity Sarah rose and waited for an explanation in a silence that became very awkward. At last the leader of the party, with such a Scottish accent that Sarah could hardly understand her, explained why they were there. 'You must think it strange,' she began, 'to see a person entirely unknown to you intrude in this manner upon your privacy.' As Sarah though it 'an unparalleled impertinence' she did not reply and the woman went on, 'You must know I am in a very delicate state of health, and my physician won't let me go to the theatre to see you, so I am to look at you here.' This explanation did not soothe Sarah's affrontedness at all, so she still said nothing while the five women, obviously expecting her to be flattered, had the nerve to sit down and stare at her. Even they, however, began to feel the silence embarrassing, because Sarah was determined not to speak, and finally they got up to go. The first woman apologized again (the others had never said a word) but Sarah, usually so considerate, really thought this was too rude, and refused to help her out. 'I was in no humour to overlook such insolence,' she said, 'and so let her depart in silence.'

All the fruits of success were not so unpalatable. The King and

Above: Sarah's father and
mother, Mr and Mrs Roger
Kemble
Left: Her eldest brother, John
Kemble

Above: The Trial Scene in *Henry VIII*. This painting by G. H. Harlow
shows Sarah as Queen Katherine with John Kemble (seated left),
Charles Kemble (seated behind table) and Stephen Kemble as Henry
VIII
Below left: Sarah as Euphrasia in *The Grecian Daughter*
Right: As Isabella in *The Fatal Marriage*

Three more of Sarah's most famous parts: *Above left:* Lady Macbeth; *above right:* Jane Shore; and, *below,* Constance in *King John*

By His **MAJESTY's COMPANY**
At the Theatre Royal in Drury-Lane,
This present MONDAY, May 27, 1776,
Will be presented a TRAGEDY, call'd.

KING RICHARD the THIRD.

King Richard by Mr. **GARRICK**,
(Being his First Appearance in that Character these 4 Years)
Richmond by Mr. **PALMER**,
Buckingham by Mr. **JEFFERSON**,
Treſſel by Mr. **DAVIES**,
Lord Stanley by Mr. BRANSBY,
Norfolk by Mr. HURST,
Catesby by Mr. PACKER,
Prince Edward by Miſs P. HOPKINS,
Duke of York Maſter PULLEY, Lord Mayor Mr GRIFFITHS,
Ratcliffe by Mr. WRIGHT, Lieutenant by Mr. FAWCETT,
King Henry by Mr. **REDDISH**,
Lady Anne (First Time) Mrs. **SIDDONS**,
Dutcheſs of York by Mrs. **JOHNSTON**,
Queen by Mrs. **HOPKINS**.
To which will be added

The DEVIL to PAY.

Sir John Loverule by Mr. **VERNON**,
Jobſon by Mr. **MOODY**,
Lady Loverule by Mrs. **JOHNSTON**,
Nell by Mrs. **WRIGHTEN**.
Ladies are deſired to ſend their Servants a little after 5 to keep Places, to prevent Confuſion.
The Doors will be opened at Half after FIVE o'Clock
To begin exactly at Half after SIX o'Clock. Vivant Rex & Regina
To-morrow, (by particular Deſire) BRAGANZA, with Bon Ton, or High Life above Stairs,
(Being the laſt Time of performing them this Seaſon.)
And Dancing by Mr. SLINGSBY and Signora PACINI.

Sarah's first season at Drury Lane – a Bill announcing her appearance as Lady Anne in *Richard III. Above:* The interior of the Drury Lane Theatre of the day

Queen, George III and Queen Charlotte, who had become great admirers of hers, invited her to Buckingham Palace. It was rare for them to see a tragedy, they preferred lighter entertainment, but they had heard so much about the wonderful young actress at Drury Lane that they had been to see her and were so impressed that they actually went to every play in which she appeared. The Queen's only criticism was that she was almost too moving; on occasion Her Majesty had been seen to turn her back completely on the stage because she could not bear to look any more.

To Sarah's astonishment they appointed her Preceptress in English Reading to the Princesses. What this great (though unpaid) honour involved Sarah did not know; she had no idea what her duties would be, but she accepted gracefully and immediately after the appointment was announced she was invited to give a Reading to the King and Queen themselves.

Always nervous on first nights she found this a most intimidating ordeal. To begin with she had to wear a ceremonial 'sack' with very wide hoops, and treble ruffles and lappets, a sort of court dress for ladies, which she hated. Then she had to go alone. Luckily for her, when she arrived and had to wait some time in the ante-room she did find some people she knew. Then the King came in. He was pulling a little basket chair behind him in which Princess Amelia, his youngest daughter who was three years old, was sitting. The King went over to speak to some other people and Princess Amelia, getting out of the chair, made straight for the tallest and prettiest person in the room, attracted too by some flowers Sarah was wearing in the front of her dress. Sarah thought she was sweet and wanted to kiss her, but when she said so to someone near, Amelia, well trained in her royal position, drew back her head and stuck out her fat little hand to be kissed. Sarah hid her amusement and the tall, stately and beautiful Mrs Siddons gravely and dutifully stooped and kissed the podgy hand of the fat, blonde little girl.

The Queen came in then, dumpy and plain, but perfectly sure of herself, and invited Sarah to begin her reading. Feeling extremely nervous Sarah did so. At every interval in the reading the Queen kept asking her to take some refreshment in the next room and Sarah kept on refusing. She said afterwards she would have stood reading till she dropped rather than have to walk out backwards because with her awkward dress and the highly polished floor she was terrified of falling down, and even she could hardly have kept her dignity if she had fallen flat on her back.

It was not only Society people and the Court who made a fuss of Sarah – all the fashionable portrait painters in London wanted to paint her, and in time she did sit for them all. Romney, Gainsborough, Reynolds and Lawrence, besides a number of other less well known artists all painted pictures of her. Lawrence, of course, had been the first. And this year he painted her as Zara in *The Mourning Bride*. He was thirteen at the time.

Sheridan and his partners, rejoicing in their find, determined to cash in on her popularity and they made Sarah play an average of three times a week all through the season. This often meant three different plays in one week, with the necessary rehearsals, and considering how emotional and exacting Sarah's parts were it was a heavy programme. Her popularity grew greater and greater and at her second benefit there had been such a rush for seats that six rows of the pit had to be turned into boxes. People gave as much as ninety guineas for a side box and seventy for an upper one. Sarah's takings from it were £650. After the hard years before, this was wonderful affluence to the Siddonses and the future looked like being well assured as, of course, Sheridan had re-engaged Sarah for the next season.

10   Irish Tour

After a tiring season and with a good sum of money in the bank it might have been expected that Sarah would take a good holiday – she had certainly earned it – but both she and William had been poor too long to count on getting money without working for it. Making hay while they could was their idea, and as soon as the Drury Lane season ended they set off for Ireland.

They went with a party – Fanny Kemble, William and Priscilla Brereton (Mrs Brereton had been the Miss Hopkins who played small parts during Sarah's first season at Drury Lane) and Francis Aickin. They were a congenial company except that William Brereton had lately started to become rather strange, at times moody and at others given to violent fits of rage. No one realized that these were the first signs of the madness that finally caused his death.

Sarah had never been on the sea before and looked forward to the whole adventure with mixed feelings. She liked new experiences and she was longing to see John who they were joining in Dublin, but she did not know how good a sailor she would be. She thoroughly enjoyed the journey to Holyhead through Wales and fell in love with the Welsh mountains, but the sea looked unpleasantly rough when they got on board, and it got rougher and rougher. Fanny was terrified and so was Mrs Brereton. Sarah was frightened too, but it was 'a pleasing terror'. She felt herself 'in the hands of a great and powerful God whose mercy is over all His works' and that the tremendous waves were a wonderful manifestation of God's power.

She was not able to stay on deck all the crossing. 'I was dreadfully sick,' she wrote to the Whalleys, 'and so were my poor sister and Mrs Brereton. Mr Siddons was pretty well; and here, my dear friends, let me give you a little wholesome advice; allways (you see I have forgot to spell) go to bed the instant you go on board, for by lying horizontally, and keeping very quiet, you cheat the sea of half its influence.'

It was half-past twelve at night before they got into Dublin, and then they had an hour and a half in the Custom Officer's room (which was like a dungeon, Sarah said) having their baggage examined. When at last they were free from officialdom they found to their horror that as it was so late they could not get a coach nor even a sedan chair, and worse still, no hotel or lodging-house in Dublin would take in a woman. It was pouring with rain and they trailed about the streets, a weary, bedraggled party, still suffering from the after-effects of sea-sickness, till nearly two-thirty, looking for somewhere to stay. They all took a very poor view of Ireland; a country where such customs were possible was barbaric. 'A pretty beginning, but these people are a thousand years behind us in every respect,' was Sarah's·comment.

In the end, dropping with exhaustion, they did find somewhere to stay. William Brereton's father had booked a bed for him (not, apparently for his wife, too!) and they went to this house. At first the landlady refused to take them in, but she was persuaded to change her mind and let them sleep the rest of that night there anyway.

They all felt slightly better after a sleep, short as it was, and breakfast next morning, but the problem of where to stay had not been solved when they went down to the Smock Alley Theatre, to meet the manager, Richard Daly. He had the unenviable reputation of being one of the most unscrupulous men in the theatrical business, though on this occasion he offered Sarah, or William acting for her, good terms. She was to play twelve times in Dublin and after expenses, estimated at £60 had been subtracted, was to get half the receipts of each evening she performed.

They did find somewhere to stay, but Sarah never liked Ireland. She thought 'the City of Dublin a sink of filthiness . . . The noissome smells, and the multitudes of shocking and most miserable objects' made her resolve never to stir out except on business. She did not like the people either. She thought they were 'all ostentation and insincerity and in their ideas of finery very like the French, but not so cleanly'. Irish exuberance and sudden savagery did not appeal to her at all, and she had very little sympathy with the intense patriotism of the Irish. 'I always acknowledge myself obliged to them, but

I cannot love them,' she wrote. She did not care for Irish hospitality either because she said it simply consisted in making people eat and drink far more than they wanted.

Irish audiences, in their turn, though they admired her acting, did not like her personally as English ones did. Warm-hearted and exuberant themselves, they thought her unnecessarily cold and dignified and never saw the friendly, kind and amusing side of her. They were never really on the same wavelength. Sarah did not like being jostled as she often was, and when a rough Irishman yelled out to her from the pit, 'Sally, me jewel, how are ye?' she did not know how to reply.

She opened her season in Dublin as Isabella in *The Fatal Marriage*, with John playing opposite her. They loved being together again and it was, in fact, the start of a long partnership. John was not as talented as she was, and never so popular, but he was much more than just competent, and they made an excellent team.

The whole Kemble family was now well to the fore in the theatre; other actors thought rather too much so. Sarah, Fanny and Elizabeth were at Drury Lane, John was about to play there, and Stephen was billed to play Othello at Covent Garden at the start of the next season.

In spite of not being so popular, and of meeting a good deal more rudeness and criticism in Ireland than she had in England, the tour was a great financial success. Her twelve nights in Dublin brought her in £1,000 and when she went on to Cork she made a further £700. She tried to fit in an extra night in Dublin because she wanted to give the proceeds to the debtors in the Marshalsea Prison, but it could not be done. She was always anxious to help this cause; she and William had had hard times themselves and knew how difficult it could be to pay debts.

When she got back to London, Sheridan opened the Drury Lane season again with *The Fatal Marriage*. It was a Command performance. The fact that the King and Queen had asked for it ensured a full house, though the takings were no better than usual, worse in fact, because so much space had to be given up for the Royal boxes. There were three; their Majesties sat in one which was swathed and looped in crimson velvet and gold, with gold cords, tassels and valances, while the princesses sat in one to the right under a canopy of blue satin and the Prince of Wales's box on the left had a canopy of blue velvet with silver fringes and tassels. In a dark blue Geneva velvet suit, heavily trimmed with gold lace, the Prince was a much grander figure than his father, who was only wearing a 'plain suit of Quaker coloured clothes with gold buttons.' The Queen was in white satin, with a headdress glittering with diamonds, and the two princesses in rose-and-white and blue-and-white figured silks. Everyone else in the theatre was as magnificently dressed as possible and the hooped skirts, powdered heads, sumptuous and gorgeous materials, jewels, fans, feathers and lace looked brilliant under the glittering chandeliers with their many candles.

It was rather strange that during the whole of the first successful season at Drury Lane, Sheridan had not tried her out in any of Shakespeare's plays. Some of the jealous actresses began to say she did not dare to act in them because she did not want to invite comparisons with the other famous actresses of the past. Sarah and Sheridan took notice of this nonsense and on 3 November she appeared as Isabella in *Measure for Measure*. This is never an easy part to make sympathetic because Shakespeare has made Isabella the kind of woman who will not make the smallest compromise with what she thinks wrong. A woman who would rather let her brother die than be unchaste herself can easily seem priggishly cold and selfish. But Sarah's Isabella was none of these things; she was noble, high-principled, idealistic and even fierce, but understandable and lovable as well. It was the sort of part Sarah loved to play and people raved about it.

It was about this time that Sarah met Dr Samuel Johnson. Mrs Thrale, Sarah's friend from Bath, Miss Moncton and other ladies had been telling him for some time he ought to meet the great actress. The old man – he was then 74 and died the next year–was in very bad health. He suffered from palsy, dropsy and gout, and was getting both deaf and blind, but his brain was quite unimpaired and his reputation for wisdom, wit, outspokenness, learning, eccentricities and simple goodness was as great as it had ever been. He was a formidable person and much as she wanted to meet him Sarah was nervous when she went to his lodgings in Bolt Street. Samuel Johnson's broad, heavy, slouched figure, in a rusty black coat much spotted down the front, was seated when she was announced. His large head was bent a little forward as if it were too heavy to hold up. There was no chair for her to sit on because every one was piled with books and Sarah hesitated, not knowing quite what to do. Dr Johnson got up as fast as his ailments would let him and said at once, 'Madam, you who so often occasion a want of seats to others will the more easily excuse the want of one yourself.'

He cleared a chair and they sat down together and from Sarah's account of the interview they got on very well. They discussed her parts and Johnson asked which of Shakespeare's characters she liked best. She told him she thought Queen Katharine in *Henry VIII* was the most natural. 'I think so too, ma'am,' he agreed, 'and whenever you perform it I will once more hobble out to the theatre myself.' He added, 'I am too deaf and blind to see or hear at a greater distance than the stage box, and have little taste for making myself a public gaze in so distinguished a situation.' Sarah sympathized with this and said she could easily arrange for him to have a comfortable chair at the stage-door, where he could see and hear everything without being seen himself. She meant the pass-door, between the auditorium and the stage; seated in the wings just behind this he would have heard and seen perfectly. Dr Johnson was pleased with the idea, but because of his health he was never again able to go to the theatre.

They discussed many of the great players he had seen. He said of Garrick, 'Garrick, madam, was no declaimer; there was not one of his own scene-shifters who could not have spoken *"To be, or not to be"* better than he did; yet he was the only actor I ever saw whom I could call a master both in tragedy and comedy; though I liked him best in comedy. A true conception of character, and a natural expression of it, were his distinguished excellencies.'

Sarah asked him what he had thought of Mrs Pritchard, whose reputation as a tragedy actress had been resplendent, and in whose footsteps she was following. He replied, 'Madam, she was a vulgar idiot; she used to speak of her "gownd", and she never read any part in a play in which she acted except her own. She no more thought of the play out of which her part was taken than a shoemaker thinks of the skin out of which the piece of leather of which he is making a pair of shoes is cut.' Sarah was astonished to hear this but Dr Johnson did add that when ever Mrs Pritchard appeared on the stage she seemed to be inspired by gentility and understanding.

After Sarah had gone Dr Johnson wrote an account of their meeting to Mrs Thrale. Until he met her he always spoke of her as 'that jade, Siddons', but now he hastened to make amends. In his letter he said, 'Mrs Siddons, in her visit to me, behaved with great modesty and propriety, and left nothing behind her to be censured or despised. Neither praise, nor money, the two powerful corrupters of mankind, seems to have depraved her. I shall be glad to see her again.'

He did see her quite often, as Sarah continued to visit him until

11 Calumnies

Sarah's second season at Drury Lane made her, if possible, more popular than ever. In tragedy there really seemed no part she could not play better than anyone else and what seemed particularly remarkable was that playgoers did not just see a beautiful young woman acting brilliantly, they saw a quite different young woman every time. Sarah looked different, walked differently, moved her whole body differently to suit each part, and she interpreted these parts as they had never been interpreted before.

In November Sheridan put on *The Gamester*. This play had been a favourite of Garrick's and since his retirement no actor had been considered good enough to take the male lead in it. Now John Kemble was given the chance. Sheridan was anxious for him to do it as he had already proved what a good actor he was as Hamlet. *The Gamester* was an interesting venture for Sarah, too. Belvidera, Zara, Euphrasia, Isabella were all heroines in the heroic manner; Mrs Beverley in *The Gamester* was just an ordinary woman whose husband, a feeble creature given to gambling, gets into the hands of a thoroughly wicked man who means to ruin him and seduce his wife. Gambling was the great vice of the age and anyone in an audience in 1783 could sympathize with Mrs Beverley who was practically beggared by her husband.

Sarah adored playing Mrs Beverley and audiences went mad over her, and even the other players were completely carried away by her acting. Once, in Edinburgh, in this play, an actor called Young found the agonizing grief in Sarah's voice made his own throat swell so much he could not speak. There was a long pause and he was prompted, but he still felt so like crying he could not get his words out and he was prompted again. Finally Sarah herself came up to him, touched him on the shoulder and said in a low voice, 'Mr Young, recollect yourself' and he was then able to pull himself together.

As the King had enjoyed *Measure for Measure* so much he told Sheridan he would like to see John and Sarah together in another play by Shakespeare, and it was decided to put on *King John*, with Sarah, of course, playing Constance. She spent hours studying the part. She thought it a difficult one because the actress playing it had to remember all the 'disastrous events and the betrayals that disappointed her ambition for herself and her dearly loved son Arthur' that had occurred in the play before Constance comes on. She does not appear till the third act and the moment she does she has to appear almost 'stunned with terrible surprise' as she realizes how she had been betrayed. Her first words are:

'Gone to be married – gone to swear a peace !
'False blood to false blood joined – gone to be friends !'

and Sarah maintained that unless an actress had been thinking all the time of Constance's wrongs she could not get the right feeling into her opening words.

In her notes about playing Constance she said, 'I never from the beginning of the play to the end of my part in it, once suffered my dressing-room door to be closed, in order that my attention might be constantly fixed on those distressing events which, by this means, I could plainly hear going on upon the stage, the terrible effects of which progress were to be represented by me. Moreover, I never omitted to place myself with Arthur in my hand, to hear the march, when, upon the reconciliation of England and France, they enter the gates of Angiers to ratify the contract of marriage between the Dauphin and Lady Blanche; because the sickening sounds of that march would usually cause the bitter tears of rage, disappointment, betrayed confidence, baffled ambition and, above all the agonizing feeling of maternal affection, to gush into my eyes.' When after getting herself into the right mood of rage and frustration in this way Sarah appeared, in black satin and with dishevelled hair, audiences were overwhelmed.

Constance was the most exacting part she had yet tackled, but she had another challenge a few weeks later when she took on Lady Randolph in a play called *Douglas*. It was a very popular play and Lady Randolph was usually played by Mrs Crawford, another well-known actress, who had made such a success in the part that Sarah knew her interpretation was bound to be compared with Mrs Crawford's in every line. This was particularly so as that actress had appeared as Lady Randolph only a month before in Covent Garden. It seems strange that the only two theatres in London should put on the same plays during the same season, but theatre-goers enjoyed comparing one player with another in the same part.

Douglas is a play with a melodramatic and improbable plot in which the hero, Lady Douglas's son by a former, secret marriage, is concealed at birth, turns up as a young man and has secret meetings with his mother who had thought he was dead. Lord Randolph believes him to be his wife's lover and has him murdered, and Lady Randolph commits suicide from grief.

There was one moment in *Douglas* when Mrs Crawford always gave a great scream of emotion; it was considered one of the most dramatic moments in the play and everyone wondered if Sarah's scream would electrify people in the same way. There was a breathless hush on the first night as this scene started and the great moment came nearer. Sarah was wearing a black dress and train, with a white ruff at the back which was carried round to the front and draped. Her dress had no hoops and her hair was neither powdered nor piled up in the fashionable manner as Mrs Crawford's was for Lady Randolph. (Sarah always hated hoops and said she could not play in them.) She looked beautiful and was far more appropriately dressed.

In the scene of Mrs Crawford's famous shriek, Lady Randolph is interviewing an old shepherd who says he discovered her son as a child, in a wicker basket, floating on the sea, and that he brought him to land. Lady Randolph then says 'Was he alive?' and it was on this line that Mrs Crawford gave her famous scream of mingled hope and anguish. However much it disappointed the audience, however, Sarah saw no reason for screaming. At that moment in the play Lady Randolph was sure her son was now dead, even if he had been saved as a baby from the sea, so that when she asked, 'Was he alive?' she simply said it hurriedly and incredulously. It was when the shepherd said he was that she turned upon him in an uncontrollable burst of pain and horror, thinking that he had saved the child from the sea only to kill him, and said :

'Inhuman art thou!
How couldst thou kill what waves and tempest spared?'

As she said it it was such a genuine expression of feeling that though a few old die-hards regretted the blood-chilling scream of Mrs Crawford most people were far more moved by Sarah's interpretation – it rang true.

One of the things that the Siddonses had always wanted was a house of their own, and now that they had four children growing up they wanted it even more. They were sick of lodgings and now they felt they could afford it they took a house in Gower Street, No. 14. They were delighted with it because at the back it overlooked fields and might have been in the country. The children loved it, too. Henry was nine now. According to his mother he was a well-disposed child and sensible, but awkward. Sally, though she was only eight, Sarah thought an elegant creature and Maria, four, was 'beautiful as a seraph'. Elizabeth the baby was only eighteen months old, but a pretty, intelligent child. It was the first time in their lives that Sarah and William had had a whole house of their own and they revelled in it. It made them able to do quite a lot of quiet entertaining on the nights when Sarah was not playing, giving little dinners to which they asked Mr and Mrs Thrale, Sir Joshua Reynolds, Gainsborough, Mr Fox and Mr Burke and even Mr Pitt, the new Prime Minister. All these men were theatre-goers and in the habit of visiting Sarah's dressing-room after the play so that she got to know them quite well.

It was about this time that Sir Joshua Reynolds painted his famous picture of Sarah as the Tragic Muse. Lawrence thought it was 'indubitably the finest female portrait in existence' which was warm praise from one portrait painter to another. Sarah arrived for the first sitting in a dress without hoops, made of rich, dark material and in a simple style. She wore her hair in two plaits on her shoulders. She had almost entirely given up white powder on her hair (she did occasionally use a sprinkling of red) and she was coming to like hair styles that showed the shape of her head. She liked simpler dress fashions too, and she and John were bringing in the idea of dressing plays in the clothes of the period. Up to this time no one had seen anything strange in a Greek heroine appearing in a hooped skirt with high-piled, powdered hair and beauty patches, and Garrick had played Macbeth in a tye-wig and the uniform of a General of George II all his life.

Sir Joshua approved of Sarah's appearance and with great gallantry he took her hand, led her towards the chair in which she was to sit and, in the grandiloquent way of the eighteenth century said, 'Ascend your undisputed throne, and graciously bestow upon me some good idea of the Tragic Muse.'

The throne was a large and imposing chair on a dais. Sarah mounted this and sat down and in her own words 'Instantly seated myself in the attitude in which the Tragic Muse now appears. This idea satisfied him so well that without one moment's hesitation he determined not to alter it.'

On the last sitting he wanted to add a little more colour to her face, but she persuaded him not to and when he saw the portrait framed he was glad he had taken her advice. Some of his earlier paintings had faded rather badly, but he assured her this one would remain for ever. 'And to confirm my opinion,' he added, 'here is my name; for I have resolved to go down to posterity on the hem of your garment.' He had, in fact, signed his name on the hem of her dress.

Not all the people who painted her were as courtly as Sir Joshua. When Gainsborough was making a portrait of her he worked for some time absolutely absorbed in what he was doing and then said suddenly, 'Damn it, Madam, there is no end to your nose!' All the Kembles had longish noses, but Sarah herself did not consider her nose as obvious as her jaw. She said laughingly of that, 'The Kemble jaw-bone! Why it is as notorious as Samson's!'

Much as they loved having a house of their own it did mean that Sarah gave up all idea of a summer holiday, and as soon as the Drury Lane season was over she set off, first to Edinburgh, and then to Ireland. William remained behind with the children because taking four of them around, with attendant nurses was too arduous and expensive.

Sarah found the Edinburgh audiences the stickiest she had ever known. In London people applauded freely throughout the whole play, but in Scotland they sat in complete silence till the end of the scene. To us, this seems far more sensible than continually holding up the action of the play with applause, but actors then liked to be sure of the audiences' appreciation all through. Sarah was quite disturbed by this unnerving silence. One night while playing a scene in a way that would have made English audiences hysterical, there was no response at all until suddenly, from the back of the theatre, a voice said loudly, 'That's no bad!' There was a moment more of silence and then an absolute roar of laughter, followed by thunders of applause, and this seemed to break the ice because from that moment on Edinburgh audiences became as responsive as any.

When Sarah went back to Ireland, she got in touch with Henrietta Boyle again, who was now Mrs O'Neil. The O'Neils owned Shane Castle. They were wealthy and ran their home luxuriously and of course asked Sarah to stay with them. 'I have not words,' she wrote, 'to describe the beauty and splendour of this enchanting place,' which was so lavishly run that it 'almost inspired the recollection of the Arabian Nights' entertainment.' The tables 'were served with a profusion and elegance' that Sarah had never met before, not even at Windsor or Buckingham Palace. The sideboards were covered with priceless silver and a band played throughout the meals. At the end of them the guests wandered about and picked their dessert from the 'many trees of the most exquisite fruit' in the conservatories. There were six or eight carriages that were kept simply to take guests round the huge estate.

Staying with the O'Neils was about the only pleasant time Sarah had in Ireland on this tour. She seemed to have a patch of bad luck that ran into one trouble after another. It started with a trivial disagreement with Richard Daly. In those days, when there were no directors or producers, the leading player arranged the grouping and Sarah told Daly – who was acting as well as stage managing – that in one scene his place was downstage. Daly was a handsome man and very vain and he was furious at being put in what he considered an inconspicuous place. He was determined to get his revenge and he started to do so a few days later when she was taken ill; he said she was malingering and refusing to carry out her contract. Sarah *was* ill and came back to work as soon as she could, but a lot of people believed Daly, and a few days later he had another opportunity of spreading false things about her.

They were rehearsing *Venice Preserved* and one of the actors was a man called Digges. He had not been looking well all through the rehearsal and suddenly, to everyone's consternation, he collapsed on the floor. Those near rushed to pick him up and found to their dismay that he had had a stroke. Of course the rehearsal was called off and Digges was carried out of the theatre to where he could be looked after. Though he was a drunkard and an old reprobate, he was popular, and everyone now, at any rate, felt sorry for him because it was unlikely he would ever be able to act again and he was very poor. Sarah was very sorry for him too and when Daly asked her if she would play in a benefit for him she said she would be delighted to. The only trouble was that she was leaving for Cork almost at once and she had already promised to have a benefit for the Marshalsea prison (in place of the one she had not been able to have last year), and she did not quite see how she could fit it in. Because he wanted to think the worst of her and make others think so too, Daly went straight off to Digges and said Sarah had refused point-blank to play for him. Everyone was saying how unkind it was of her when another message came from Sarah to say that, on thinking it over, she believed she ought to play for Digges and would do so. Daly's first story, however, got about.

In spite of everyone's so-called sympathy for 'poor old Digges' Sarah had the greatest trouble in getting a cast together for his benefit. Daly did very little to help and people let her down left and right. 'It was a scene of disgust and confusion,' she lamented. 'I acted Belvidera without having ever previously seen the face of one of the actors.' The benefit made a lot of money for Digges, but Sarah said it was a most 'ludicrous performance'.

It was hard, after all the trouble she had taken, to find the unscrupulous Daly telling everyone that Sarah had only changed her mind and agreed to play for Digges if she got £50 for doing so. It was quite usual to give a star a fee for a benefit, since they brought in so much more money, but the fee was never more than £30. In this case, as the poor man was ill, Sarah had not asked for, nor received, a penny.

Daly went on with his campaign against her, both in the Press and by whispering slanders. He even went so far as to beg people to hoot her from the stage because of her cruelty to poor Digges.

She got into a series of benefit muddles at this time. There was a mix up about the one she was to give for Mr Brereton. They had promised to act in each other's, but Brereton was ill when Sarah's was given and so could not take part, and she could not find a day in which to play in his. She tried very hard for him, and promised to play for £20 instead of £30, but they never could find a night that suited them both. Daly pounced on this story too – Mrs Siddons again refusing to help a fellow actor. Sarah could not understand Brereton – he could easily have put the whole thing right, but he said nothing and just looked morose and unapproachable. It was really because the poor man was becoming insane, but not realizing this she thought he was very unkind since his behaviour made many people believe Daly's slanders were true.

All this was extremely unpleasant and when Sarah got back to England she ran into more trouble there, though this had nothing to do with benefits.

When Sarah and William were in Bath they had made friends with a bookseller called Pratt. He had borrowed £500 from William to tide him over a difficult time (which had not been repaid) and he then came to London and borrowed another £10 from Sarah. When she asked for it back he took no notice and merely sent her a tragedy he had written. Sarah told him that she had had to make a rule not to read any plays for fear of giving offence to authors whose work she had not time to read and she advised Pratt to try his play with the theatre managers. She would have been swamped with plays if she had not made this rule. But Pratt was furious with her, and though he was supposed to be in love with Fanny Kemble, he said he was going to publish a poem he had written called *Gratitude* in which he made out that he was the ladder to fame which Sarah had climbed and then kicked down. How he became a ladder for her he did not say; because beyond going to the theatre when she was acting he did not do anything for her at all. Naturally relations became rather strained between them after this and when Pratt saw that he was going to get nothing out of her he took to writing the most scurrilous things he could. He also took a malicious delight in reporting all the discreditable things he could about Anne Kemble, the only one of the family who had not done well. Anne was a terrible trouble to them all because she drank heavily and was always making scenes – she loved notoriety. Sarah gave her an annuity of twenty pounds a year – it was no use giving her much money, she simply drank it – but she was almost impossible to help. She had just attracted a lot of publicity by taking poison in Westminster Abbey. She did not die – she took very good care that the dose was not lethal, but it was very distressing and embarrassing for all the Kembles. This was a wonderful opportunity for Pratt and he lost no time in exploiting it, together with all the wild stories about Digges and Brereton. As might be expected there were quite a number of people jealous of Sarah's spectacular success who were very glad to hear and spread, stories of her meanness and hard heart.

The attacks were really venomous and Sarah and William were staggered at so much malice. The latter wrote at once to Digges, asking him to publish the truth. Digges did so, but owing to bad weather the letter was delayed and in the meantime Sarah had a very unpleasant and unnerving experience.

Her opening night that Season was on 5 October in *The Gamester*. She walked on to the stage and was immediately hissed. Hoots and shouts of 'Off! Off!' were hurled at her. Digges's letter, if published, could have saved her from 'the horror of that dreadful night' but as it was it was some time before the noise died down at all. Then, just as Sarah was going to speak a man in the audience sprang up, shouting 'For heaven's sake, Madam, do not degrade yourself by an apology, for there is nothing necessary to be said.'

Sarah was grateful to 'this gallant man's solitary advocacy' of her cause, but he did not do her much actual good because before she could speak the noise broke out again and was so loud and angry that John Kemble insisted on her leaving the stage. She let him lead her back, but the shock had been so great that, calm as she had seemed on the stage, once off it she fainted. She was thankful she had not done this on the stage and that 'her persecutors had not had the gratification of beholding this weakness'. She was bitterly angry and hurt and so disgusted that though William, John and Mr Sheridan all advised her to go back on stage when the audience became calmer, in her first fury she said she would never act again. However, they managed to soothe her and at last she agreed to return. It did take a lot of courage, but when she appeared to 'her great and pleasant astonishment she was received in silence'. She stood there beautiful, brave and dignified and the audience let her speak. 'Ladies and Gentleman,' she said, 'the kind and flattering partiality which I have uniformly experienced in this place would make the present interruption distressing to me indeed, were I in the slightest degree conscious of having deserved your censure. I feel no such consciousness. The stories which have been circulated against me are calumnies. When they shall be proved to be true, my aspersors will be justified; but till then, my respect for the public leads me to be confident that I shall be protected from unmerited insult.'

Having said this as the embodiment of outraged innocence and dignity, Sarah withdrew proudly and the curtain came down. It was raised again when Aickin came on the stage to tell the audience that Sarah had played for his benefit and that the rumours about her were altogether unfounded. John tried to make Brereton do the same, but he said in an embarrassed way that as he had published a letter exonerating Sarah that morning, there was no need for him to speak. His letter had given the fact, but grudgingly, and Sarah, William and John thought he ought to have spoken up for her that night.

Sarah's behaviour appealed to the public and more or less finished the whole episode. Some cartoons were drawn of her hoarding moneybags, nicknames such as 'Lady Sarah Save-all' were given

F

her and for a few nights afterwards some trouble-makers booed her, but it died away. But some mud always sticks and even today, two hundred odd years later, the legend persists that she was stingy in her praise of others and mean with money. In fact she was very generous and large-hearted, and never turned her back on anyone if she could give them help.

12 Lady Macbeth

The public might become as enthusiastic as ever and forget that they had ever booed her, but Sarah was so hurt by all the horrible things said about her that she became quite ill. She wrote to the Whalleys, 'I have been very unhappy, now it is over I will tell you so . . . Envy, malice, detraction, all the fiends of hell have compassed me round to destroy me, but, "Blessed be God who has given me the victory, etc." . . . I have been charged with almost everything bad . . . God help them and forgive them; they know but little of me . . . But what makes the wound rankle deeper is that ingratitude, hypocrisy and perfidy have barbed the darts. But it is over . . .'

Although she got better and put it behind her as soon as she could, she felt bewildered by the malice and ingratitude people had shown. She could not imagine why anyone should say such things of her because she was always so ready to help anyone who asked her. She did not go round boasting of what she did, but in fact she often wrote to Government Ministers about people, trying to right their wrongs, or get them posts. She was always trying to get jobs for people out of work, or else helping them with money and clothes, which made it so strange to her that these hateful calumnies should ever have been started and that people who knew nothing of her private life should attack her.

She was always surprised by malice – she had so little of it in her own nature that she never expected it in other people, and she never thought how likely it was that less successful people should be jealous and ready to believe evil of her. William was attacked too. Rumours that he was unkind and unfaithful to her, founded solely on the spiteful reports of a servant dismissed for drunkenness and dishonesty, were going round and made Sarah miserable. In her letter to the Whalleys she went on, 'Our old Mary, too, whom you may remember, has proved a very viper. She has lately taken to drinking, has defrauded us of a great deal of money given her to pay the tradespeople, and in her cups has abused Mr Siddons and me beyond all bounds; I believe in my soul that all the scandalous reports of Mr Siddons's ill-treatment of me originated entirely in her. One may pay for one's experience, and the consciousness of acting rightly is a comfort that hell-born malice cannot rob us of . . .'

Nothing was going quite right at the moment, not even in the theatre because, although she had one tremendous success as Margaret of Angou in *The Earl of Warwick*, the other plays Sheridan had put on were very poor with nothing in them for her. Sheridan decided to give up new plays for the moment and put on another classic and he chose *Macbeth*.

Sarah had played this part many times since that night when she had had the horrors studying it, but she was still not satisfied with her interpretation. She knew she must put every ounce of her intelligence into it this time because she was quite aware that everyone would compare her with Mrs Pritchard, whose great part it had been. Although Dr Johnson had said Mrs Pritchard was an idiot, even he had admitted that she was an inspired idiot on the stage, and people still talked about her Lady Macbeth.

Sarah thought Lady Macbeth was more than a woman who was unscrupulously ambitious, she thought of her as a woman whose ambition was so boundless that she had become inhuman. 'In this astonishing creature one sees a woman in whose bosom the passion of ambition has almost obliterated all the characteristics of human nature,' she wrote in her notes on the character.

The play was given first on 2 February 1785 and experienced and successful as Sarah was, she was as nervous that night as she had ever been in her life. She got to the theatre early and dressed, and then told her dresser to go away. She told her not to let anyone come near her till it was time for her to go on, because she simply could not bear to see or talk to anyone. The dresser went and Sarah was left alone, trying to calm herself and think herself into Lady Macbeth. Suddenly, to her annoyance, someone knocked at the door. It was Richard Sheridan, insisting agitatedly that he must see her. Pulling her mind with difficulty from 'pondering with fearfulness' her 'first appearance in the grand, fiendish part' Sarah begged him to go away and leave her alone. Sheridan refused. He must see her

now. He could not put off what he had to say because it concerned
the play. Very much against her will Sarah let him in, hoping he
would say what he had to quickly and go away. She was irritated
at having to speak to him at all, but she could hardly believe her ears
when she heard what he had come for. He wanted her, at this
moment, just before she went on the stage, to alter the sleep-walking
scene. He had suddenly realized that she had changed the tradition,
hallowed by Mrs Pritchard, of playing the whole scene holding a
candlestick in her hand. He was quite sure audiences would not
like any change at all; she must do what Mrs Pritchard had always
done. Sarah stared at him – she was appalled. Then she refused
point-blank. She could not possibly change anything at this hour,
and if she did half the effectiveness of washing out 'the damned
spot' would be gone. Sheridan insisted. People would not like any
innovation, it would be a terrible mistake. Though she was distracted,
after all Sheridan was the manager and she usually had great confidence in his taste, she still refused to alter anything. It was far too
late to do so and in any case she considered her way of presenting a
person walking in their sleep was far more true to life than Mrs
Pritchard's.

Sheridan tried very hard to move her and they had quite a battle.
Then at last he realized, angrily, that she would not alter anything
and that he was only upsetting her. He went off muttering about the
obstinacy of women and of Sarah in particular.

It was a shocking start to a difficult part and Sarah hardly had
time to get herself in hand before she was called. But from the
moment when, dressed in black with deep red borders falling from
her shoulders to the hem of her dress, and with a white veil she
walked on reading Macbeth's letter, so absorbed in it that the illusion
that she had just walked from one room to another was complete,
the audience was gripped. The house was full. Everyone who was
anyone had tried to get seats. The politicians Fox, Wyndham and
Burke were in the front row, and so was Gibbon, at that time still
writing his *Decline and Fall of the Roman Empire*. Sir Joshua Reynolds was there too – he had designed the costume Sarah was to wear
in the sleep-walking scene.

When she got to that scene there was no doubt who was right –
she or Mrs Pritchard. She came on, dressed in white, walked rapidly
to a table, put her candle down on it and began at once to pour
imaginary water over her right hand and wash it. Before Sarah sleep-
walkers were always played with feeble, languid movements and

eyes fixed straight ahead. She did not think this true at all, she believed that in sleep-walking people move as they do when they are awake; that is their muscles respond in the usual way to their brains, and though she broke away from the convention, she made everyone believe she was walking in her sleep.

She was equally successful in the banquet scene. She believed Lady Macbeth was dying with fear, yet assuming the utmost composure . . . 'entertaining her wondering guests with frightful smiles, with over-acted attention, and with fitful graciousness; painfully yet incessantly, labouring to divert their attention from her husband' and she played her like that. In the end Lady Macbeth can stand this so-called feasting no more, and when she said,

> 'at once good night;
> Stand not upon the order of your going,
> But go at once,'

a member of the audience noted that at this point Sarah descended 'in great eagerness', her 'voice almost choked with anxiety to prevent their questioning'; her 'alarm and hurry' were 'rapid and convulsive' as if she was 'afraid Macbeth should tell of the murder of Duncan'.

It was such brilliant acting that people could not take their eyes off her or look at anyone else when she was on the stage. One man said, 'Of Lady Macbeth there is not a great deal in this play, but the wonderful genius of Mrs Siddons makes it the whole.'

When she got back to her dressing-room, with the thunders of applause still going on, Sheridan hurried round to see her, to tell her eagerly how glad he was that she had been obstinate. She was perfectly right about the candle, and he apologized.

Sarah had not really come out of the part and hardly took in what he was saying and even when he had gone she was still in a daze. She began to unfasten the white cloak she was wearing and as she did so she kept repeating to herself, 'Here's a smell of blood still!' and then started to rub her hands. Her dresser took her words literally. 'Dear me, Ma'am,' she said, 'how very hysterical you are tonight; I protest and vow, ma'am, it is not blood, but rose-pink and water; I saw the property man mix it with my own eyes.' Sarah caught the woman's anxious eyes fixed on her and suddenly realized what she was saying. She shook herself free of the part, laughed and came back to normal.

The whole of London buzzed with Mrs Siddons's playing of Lady Macbeth – probably no actress even now has ever surpassed her in this part. Her contemporaries thought she had reached her peak, which made them astonished that the next Shakespeare play she was to appear in was *Othello*. Sarah Siddons as Desdemona! That tall, dark creature who could play a fiend like Lady Macbeth so superlatively well, act a gentle, faithful sweet young wife! Impossible! Of course it was true that she was still only twenty-nine and a half and as slender as a young girl, and of course it was also true that she had a sort of large-hearted, almost child-like simplicity about her which was very suitable for Desdemona, but after such a transcendent Lady Macbeth quite a number of people thought she was attempting something she could never manage.

Sarah had no doubts. She did not much like playing women who were trivial and stupid, but Desdemona was great in her love and constancy and she was delighted to have a change from the horrible Lady Macbeth.

Even the doubtful admitted that she was an enchanting Desdemona, and in her own inimitable way she made herself look much smaller and more frail. Two hundred years later we don't know how she did this; we have just to accept it as a sign of her greatness. An actor who played with her when she was Margaret of Angou said that she looked so like a giantess when she appeared in the centre arch at the back of the stage that it had taken his breath away, and yet this same woman could look slender and small and frail a few weeks later.

Sarah was thrilled with her notices, especially after all the horrible things the papers had been saying about her lately. One said, 'In this wonderful transition from Lady Macbeth to the bride of Othello, Mrs Siddons has shown her genius to be a star of the first magnitude.'

She was not able to repeat her triumph of Desdemona at once. All the next day she said she felt very stiff and she was sure it was because the bed she had been murdered on was damp. The next day she was worse, all her joints ached intolerably and instead of going down to the theatre to repeat her triumph she had to go to bed, where she remained for a fortnight, with a bad attack of rheumatism. William was outraged and spoke his mind very forcibly to the stage manager.

She recovered in time to play in a flop which even her brilliant acting could not save, and then Sheridan announced that she was to play Rosalind in *As You Like It*. Even though she had been such an excellent Desdemona, he was unwise to give her this part. For one thing another actress, Dora Jordan, had just played it enchant-ingly and for another, though Sarah liked the part she was not at all suited to a light-hearted girl like Rosalind. It is strange that she did like it, because she hated appearing in boy's clothes. She was terribly prudish about this and wrote to the artist Hamilton asking him to design a costume for her that was not too boyish. Between them they hashed up something that Sarah thought very suitable and decent, but everyone else deplorable. She wore hessian boots and a man's coat, but instead of trousers a sort of short apron in front and a skirt behind. It is hard to visualize this extraordinary garment, and harder still to imagine how Sarah could have been such a fool as to wear it. It did not give her a chance and though some people said she was quite good, most critics thought she made an error in attempting Rosalind.

13 Success Continues

Although Sarah was not at her best as a comedy actress on the stage she was extremely funny when she entertained friends at home. It is said that she was wonderful as Anthony Absolute and she was renowned for her lugubrious recitation of a popular ballad *Billy Taylor* and equally funny when she read scenes or told stories.

Rosalind was her last play that season. Though she was now getting £24 10s. a week, and making a lot of money from her benefits, she could not rest and went on tour again immediately. It was an exhausting tour, though worth it financially. Country audiences were just as enthusiastic about her as London ones and she played to packed houses wherever she went. Her manager for the tour was Tate Wilkinson, a great friend of hers. No woman smoked then, of course, but Sarah took snuff and she particularly liked Tate Wilkinson's brand. 'I never think of you,' she wrote, 'but I wish to be regaling with you over a pinch of your most excellent Irish snuff, which I have never had a snift of, but in idea, since I left York.' Snuff and Sarah do not seem to go together but she had a quarter of an ounce delivered every week from Messrs Fribourge and Treyer and hated to be without it.

The tour, like all her tours, was a great success, though at times odd things happened and some things went wrong. At Leeds, one night, she sent the call-boy out to fetch her a glass of porter – a kind of beer. The boy, who must have been an unusually dim-witted child, got back when Sarah was in the middle of the sleep-walking scene in *Macbeth* and instead of waiting till it was over, marched on to the stage and presented the porter to her. Sarah tried to wave him away, but he was too stupid to go and when he was at last called off by someone in the wings, he had completely wrecked the scene – the whole audience were roaring with laughter. Another time, also at Leeds, Sarah was about to drink some poison – one of the dramatic moments of the play – when a voice from the gallery shouted, 'Soop it opp, lass!' She tried to keep a straight face, but could not; she simply had to laugh.

In the May of this year, 1785, both Elizabeth and Fanny married. Elizabeth had only had two seasons at Drury Lane and then gone back to the provinces, where she met her husband, Charles Edward Whitlock, the manager of the Theatre Royal, Newcastle upon Tyne. Soon after their marriage the Whitlocks went to America, and there Elizabeth at once became a star, partly because there was not much competition and partly because of her name. Fanny, who had a number of admirers, married Francis Twiss, a theatre critic. Sarah and William were thankful she had sent the ungrateful Pratt packing. Another theatre critic, Mr Steevens had wanted to marry Fanny and he never forgave her for turning him down. He was a spiteful man, very vain, and he took every opportunity of writing petty and unkind things about her. He could not do her much harm because she left the stage when she married, and anyway Fanny did not worry about his hatefulness, she and Francis Twiss were far too happy. They lived in London at first, but later she opened a school for girls in Bath.

The autumn season that year was not as brilliantly successful for Sarah as usual. There was a fashion for comedies for a time in London and neither she nor Sheridan could find any good new ones that suited her. In some ways she did not mind, because she was expecting another baby and so was glad not to have to work as hard as usual. George Siddons was born on 26 December and was 'as healthy and lovely as an angel', Sarah said. After four girls in a row she was delighted to have another boy.

She went back to the theatre remarkably soon after George's birth, though she did not try any new part until 15 May, when she played Ophelia to John's Hamlet. Even with the memory of Desdemona there were sceptics who could not believe she would be good as the frail-looking, wafty Ophelia, but being Sarah, of course she managed it easily. She could be as frail-looking as she liked and she was so moving in the mad scenes that the actress playing Gertrude completely forgot her words, she was so upset and electrified by the look Sarah gave her.

Sheridan and Sarah were always looking for new plays, but the public were perfectly happy to see her in old ones. Both in London and the provinces whenever she acted the theatre was packed. This meant the money came in so well that by the 1785-6 season Sarah found she had done what she always wanted to do – made £10,000 to invest. From now on even if she died or had to give up acting William and the children were safe.

Having the money behind her made her feel she could relax a little and in the summer of 1787 she took a long holiday and did no work at all. Mrs Thrale, whose husband had died, had remarried and was now Mrs Piozzi. She asked the whole family to stay part of the summer with her, and when they left her they went on to Nuneham, the home of the Earl and Countess of Harcourt. Lady Harcourt was one of Sarah's greatest admirers and had also become a very great friend.

The next excitement in the Kemble family was John's wedding. For years he had been in love with the enchanting, stammering Mrs Inchbald (now a widow) and everyone, Sarah included, expected him to marry her. No one knows why he did not ask her. Years after he was married he asked her one day when she was saying who she would, or would not have married, 'Well, Mrs Inchbald, would you have had me?' 'Dear heart,' she said, with her delightful stammer, turning her sweet, sunny face up to him, 'I'd have jumped at you!'

All his family were surprised when he announced he was going to marry Priscilla Brereton, the widow of the poor man who had gone insane. No one had any idea he was in love with her – if he was. He was certainly not an ardent wooer. Priscilla herself was taken by surprise too. One day John chucked her under the chin and told her that she would soon hear of something to her advantage. By the way he said it she thought he meant something serious, but was not sure what. Her mother said it was a proposal and apparently it was, because a fortnight later they were married. John behaved as strangely over his wedding – not at all like a man in love. He did turn up in time for the service, but it turned out he had made no preparation for the wedding dinner – it was his job to do this – nor for any festivity, he only said when asked he supposed they should dine at home. One of the guests was scandalized by this and asked them all home to dinner with her.

John's peculiar behaviour continued. The bride and the guests arrived for the meal but to their astonishment he had disappeared without saying where he was going. No one, not even Priscilla, knew where he was, nor even if he meant to turn up. They did not like to start without him, but as the bride was acting that evening – in itself strange on her wedding day – they could not wait too long. Finally he did turn up and had dinner, but even then he did not go with his new wife to the theatre; he preferred to spend the evening playing with her young brothers and sisters, until he went off to fetch her from Drury Lane. The odd thing was that in spite of this start it was a very happy marriage. Even if they were not madly in love they were very fond of each other and the marriage was completely successful.

It was not long after John's wedding that the Greatheeds came into Sarah's life again. Bertie Greatheed, the little boy she used to read to at Guy's Cliffe, wrote a play called *The Regent* and sent it to Sarah to read. He had had her in mind as he wrote it and of course, he wanted her to play in it. Sarah was delighted to hear from the Greatheeds again, but unfortunately she thought the play deplorable. 'It certainly has some beautiful poetry,' she wrote to the Whalleys, 'but the plot of the poor young man's piece is very lame and the characters very, very ill-sustained in general, more particularly the lady, for whom the author had me in his eye. This woman is one of those monsters (I think them) of perfection, who is an angel before her time and is so entirely resigned to the will of heaven, that (to a very mortal like myself) she appears to be the most provoking piece of still life one ever had the misfortune to meet.'

Sarah was outspoken to Bertie about the play and hoped that she had put him off it, but to her dismay he said at once that it would be no trouble at all to alter it and he would be delighted to do so if she would play what she called 'the milksop lady'. He had to make several more alterations before she finally, and reluctantly, agreed to act in it. It was put on on 20 March 1788. Sarah was taken ill on the second night and though the play did get acted several times more, it was a flop. Bertie believed that but for her unlucky illness the play would have run a long time and Sarah did not disillusion him. She was thankful to get out of the matter so easily, without spoiling her friendship with the Greatheeds.

14 Queen Katharine

William and Sarah had a great grief that spring; their youngest daughter, Elizabeth, died when she was not quite six. She was an unusually engaging and lovable child, 'fair as wax, with very blue eyes and the sweetest tuneful voice you ever heard', Sarah said of her, adding that she was the most entertaining creature in the world.

But happy or unhappy, actresses have to go on rehearsing and acting, and on 5 May, only three weeks after Elizabeth's death, Sarah appeared in Dryden's *All for Love* – a play about Cleopatra. Although Sarah was beautiful enough to play this fabulous woman, no two people could have been more unlike in character, and though she could become on the stage a woman as unlike her real self as Lady Macbeth, she could not play a seductive siren. It was never one of her great successes.

Early in this summer King George III had his first bout of insanity. Sarah always believed she was one of the first people to see signs of it. During that May she was bidden to Windsor and while she was there the king, in a very odd way, gave her a piece of paper with nothing on it but his name. His manner was so peculiar as he did this that it almost seemed as if he were inviting her to fill up the paper with anything she wanted in money or patronage. It was so strange that for a moment Sarah wondered if he was thinking of making love to her, but she hastily put this idea from her. She neither would nor could believe it, because not only was the King a most devoted husband, but she was known everywhere as a most devoted wife. She took the paper but did not know what to do with it, and after some thought decided to show it to the Queen privately, without telling anyone else. Queen Charlotte thought very highly of Sarah for her discretion; a lot of people would have rushed round spreading the wildest rumours and making as much as possible out of it.

Sarah kept going till the end of the Drury Lane season, but when it was over she felt so exhausted that she decided not to go on tour at all that summer. Instead she went back to Guy's Cliffe, to stay with the Greatheeds for several weeks.

Sarah had certainly plenty to make her nervy and depressed that summer. She was not only sad about Elizabeth's death, but she was distracted by matters at the theatre. The trouble there was caused by Sheridan; no one could get him to pay their salaries. Drury Lane was full almost every night, salaries were not excessive and Sheridan was known to be making a lot of money, but there never seemed to be any cash to pay anyone. Sheridan, brilliant playwright and theatre manager as he was was becoming far more interested in his other career, that of a Member of Parliament. He was absorbed in the Impeachment of Warren Hastings. The whole of educated England felt passionately about this and the debates in the House of Commons were followed avidly by everyone. Sheridan was in the House all the time, taking part in and listening to the debates, and less and less at the theatre. He was also drinking heavily and becoming quite irresponsible towards his players. They all found him infuriating to deal with. When he did come to the theatre he was usually drunk and always in a hurry. He would not listen to anyone, found fault with everything and dashed off again without giving any of the exasperated cast a chance to air their complaints and demand their arrears. And yet, though he infuriated them so much, when he chose he had such charm that they found themselves putting up with his intolerable behaviour and continuing to play for him even without their pay.

It was not only Sheridan who was causing life at the theatre to be unpleasant. King, the actor who had reported on Sarah to Garrick all those years ago at Cheltenham was responsible for the day-to-day running of Drury Lane and there were constant complaints about the way he did this. Sheridan, who was getting tired of King wanted John Kemble to take over this job. This leaked out and feuds and factions immediately raged making just the sort of atmosphere Sarah loathed. When the season was over King resigned in a fury and wrote to the papers putting his point of view. 'Should anyone ask me what *was* my post at Drury Lane, and, if I was not manager, who was I, should be forced to answer . . . *"I don't know . . . I can't tell* – I can only once more positively assert that I was *not manager*; for I had not the power by any agreement, nor indeed had I the wish, to approve, or reject, any new dramatic work; the liberty of engaging, encouraging, or discharging any one performer – nor sufficient authority to command the cleaning of a coat, or adding, by way of decoration, a yard of copper lace; both of which, it must be allowed, were often much wanted." '

If what King said was true the stage manager of Drury Lane did have a thankless task, but it seems to have been his own inefficiency that made things so hopeless, because when John took the work over he managed to get all the reins into his own hands and keep them there. He had Sarah to back him up, of course, and as she was by far the most important person in the whole company this helped, but John was, in every way, a much bigger man than King, and a man with much more definite ideas. He was a perfectionist – every detail of every play had to be right. He insisted on a meticulous accuracy in the text and as he was collecting a magnificent library of dramatic first editions he knew what the right text was. The word accuracy he insisted on benefited the whole theatrical world, but his emphasis on detail (even the quarterings on Heraldic banners had to be correct) led to scenery becoming more and more elaborate and a far more important part of the presentation than it had, so that by the next century, and indeed right up to recent times, audiences expected and demanded very realistic and elaborate settings and began to pay more attention to this than to the acting. It also meant that plays became much more expensive to stage.

John's first chance of trying out his new methods came in his production of Shakespeare's *Henry VIII* on 26 November. Every detail had to be right and he studied books and pictures to be sure of getting the costumes and sets authentic. He also got a brilliant company to play it, with Sarah of course as Katharine of Aragon. The whole play, and particularly Sarah's Queen Katharine, created such furore that it even competed with the Trial of Warren Hastings in general interest. Sarah made the Queen a person of courage and grandeur and of generosity, and from her first entrance, when she came in to the court and knelt before Henry she caught and held the sympathy of all audiences. She was playing this part once when one of the actors came off the stage agitated and perspiring, and wiping his forehead said to another, 'That woman plays as if the thing were in earnest. She looked at me so through and through with her black eyes that I would not for the world meet her on the stage again.'

Sarah was almost at her best in the scene when Katharine is dying. She looked desperately ill and she was fretful, restless and unable to find a comfortable position. She kept having her pillows moved, or leaning forward with her hands on her knees as if seeking some way of easing her pain and discomfort. She kept pulling at her clothes with her hands and yet through it all kept Katharine's natural queen-liness and courage and goodness. It was a most brilliant portrayal and never forgotten by anyone who saw it.

Katharine was not Sarah's only great success that season – she played Volumnia in *Coriolanus*. At thirty-three she looked a little young to be the mother of a grown man, but she played it so well that this was forgotten. One of her best moments was the scene of Coriolanus's triumphal entry. She came on to the stage as part of the procession but walking alone, marching and beating time to the music. Someone who was there that first night said, 'She towered above all around her and almost reeled across the stage; her very soul, as it were, dilating and rioting in its exultation, until her action lost all grace, and, yet, became so true to nature, so picturesque and so descriptive, that pit and gallery sprang to their feet, electrified by the transcendent execution of the conception.' It was like Sarah to make the 'intoxication of joy' like a real intoxication and to lurch across the stage, out of time with the music and 'appearing' said another eyewitness, 'to reap all the glory of that procession to her-self'.

She had to be content with these two outstanding successes for the rest of the season because the other plays she appeared in were so bad it was considered remarkable she kept them running as long as she did. Ill-advisedly she played Juliet too, in *Romeo and Juliet*. She was too old to play fifteen convincingly, and too tall and grand for Shakespeare's Juliet anyway, though some people liked her in a few scenes.

She felt well enough that summer to go on tour again, and during that tour she took up another art which thrilled her. She was at Birmingham and was doing some shopping in a place that dealt in statuary when she noticed a very bad head and shoulders of herself. The shopman saw she was interested in it, but did not recognize her and hurried across and told her it was 'the likeness of the greatest and most beautiful actress ever seen in the world'. Sarah was gratified at his compliment, but thought as a likeness of her it was deplorable and was sure she could model a better one herself. She bought the bust and went home and ordered some clay at once and was soon so fascinated with modelling that it became one of her great hobbies for the rest of her life.

When that summer came to an end the Siddonses took a great decision – Sarah should not go back to Drury Lane. Sheridan was more hopeless than ever and they agreed Sarah should not play for him again till he paid what he owed her. Though Sheridan was furious he took the line that he could get on perfectly well without her if she wanted to stay away she could. It was a blow to John, but he really agreed; he believed it might bring Sheridan to his senses and benefit them all. It was about time something did.

15 Lawrence

Sarah was not out of work, she toured again. Provincial theatre managers all clamoured for her and she got as much acting as she wanted. The following summer she and William went to Calais to visit Sally and Maria who had gone to a finishing school there early in 1789. The girls had only been there a few months when the French Revolution began with the fall of the Bastille in July. Horrified as people in England were by this, there was no talk of bringing Sally and Maria home, nor were Sarah and William in the least afraid of any danger when they went to visit them. 'I set out with Mr S., Miss Wynn and her brother for Calais,' Sarah wrote to Lady Harcourt, 'and found my dear girls quite well and improved in their person, and (I am told) in their French.' Reading history one imagines that the whole of France was in a revolutionary uproar, with riots and guillotines everywhere, but the Siddonses seem to have seen nothing of it because they took the girls out in the ordinary way. Among other places they went to Lisle, and being Siddonses went at once to the theatre there. 'Though I knew nothing of the language the acting was so really good that it gave me very great pleasure,' Sarah wrote.

She enjoyed her trip abroad, but she was still not well and when they returned from France she and William went to Sandgate for her health. 'I have bathed four times,' she wrote to Lady Harcourt, 'and I believe I shall persevere, for Sir Lucas Pepys says my disease is entirely nervous. I believe I am better, but I get on so slowly that I cannot speak as yet with much certainty. I still suffer a good deal. Mr Siddons leaves me here for a fortnight while he goes to town on business, and my spirits are so bad that I live in terror of being alone.'

Later that summer she and William took Nuneham Rectory, in Oxfordshire, near the Harcourts' country place. Mrs Piozzi came to stay with them. She was worried about Sarah, whom she thought was in a highly nervous state, but while she was there they had an agitating experience which might have upset anyone. According to her Sarah had not properly recovered from a miscarriage when they had a terrific thunderstorm 'which', she wrote in her diary, 'killed a woman within our view, & fired ten shocks of a neighbouring Farmer's Corn under the very windows. Our young girls, Cecilia and Miss Siddons fell into Fits, the Baby Boy George not 5 years old was from Home, gone o'merrymaking with our servants to some village not far off – the Mother became a real picture of Despair, supposing him to be killed by Lightning . . .' George came home safely and the girls recovered from their hysterics, but Mrs Piozzi, according to herself, was the only person to cope with everyone, Sarah was quite incapable. For anyone not well and in a nervy state to start with such an afternoon would be shattering and no doubt Sarah was not as self-controlled as usual.

Her health did not get much better as summer went on and towards the end of it she went to Harrogate to try if the waters would do her any good. Sheridan had found, to his annoyance, that he could not get on without her – no one filled the theatre as she did – and he had to humble himself and ask her to return. In the end, though wondering if it was foolish, Sarah and William agreed she should, though Sarah said she could not possibly do so in September. In fact she did not expect to be well enough to start acting again until after Christmas. It was not Drury Lane theatre she was to return to, but the Opera House in the Haymarket; Sheridan had had to take that because Drury Lane, which had had nothing substantial done to it for over a hundred years and was no longer considered safe, was to be rebuilt.

To everyone's dismay Sheridan commissioned Henry Holland to rebuild it and make it far larger. His company thought him mad. No one dared to think what it would cost. He had raised £160,000 to rebuild it (an enormous sum of money for those days) but everyone connected with the theatre was sure it would be more expensive even than that because both Henry Holland and Sheridan had such grandiose ideas.

Besides moving theatres Sarah also moved house. The Siddonses left Gower Street and moved to 54 Great Marlborough Street, which was to be their home for several years. Only the two boys, Henry and George were at home – the girls were still in France. Henry, who had just left Charterhouse, now announced that he wanted to go on the stage. His parents were disappointed. They wanted him to go to the university with a view to taking Holy Orders, but he was insistent he wanted to be an actor. Sarah and William were not at all sure he had the talent, so they compromised. Henry was to go to Paris first, to learn French. While there he might see the famous French actor Lekain and then return to England and if he still wanted to, try his luck on the stage.

Apparently the fact that the Revolution was at its height did not worry anyone, even though the stories of what was happening in France were becoming more and more horrible. Pitiful streams of refugees, with their terrible tales, kept arriving. People in England were horrified. Nowadays we are used to atrocity stories, but at the end of the eighteenth century ordinary men and women believed that human beings had become too civilized to do such things to each other. Especially in France which had always claimed to be the centre of cultured civilization. When the news of Louis XVI's death on 21 January 1793 came through, all the theatres closed for a night as a sign of mourning and respect.

This decided Sarah and William to bring their daughters home. France was no place to live in for the moment, not for girls anyway. Sally was now seventeen and Maria nearly fourteen. They were both pretty. Sally had much of her mother in her, though most people did not think her as beautiful. She had Sarah's eyes and she was like her in expression, a mixture of sweetness and openness. She had Sarah's simple, uncomplicated nature too, but she had none of her mother's genius and was quieter and more reserved. Mrs Piozzi admired her looks more than Maria's, but she was always particularly fond of Sally, and most people thought Maria the prettier. At fourteen she was enchanting and later she became as beautiful as her mother as a girl, with enormous dark eyes and dark hair.

The girls had brought back all the new, French, Jacobin fashions; skimpy dresses with very high waists, self-coloured stocking and even drawers – the latter considered by everyone as very shocking. Most extraordinary of all to the Siddonses' friends was the way they did their hair. Who could ever have imagined that girls would want to cut off their plaits and curls and have their hair cut short into a tousled mop?

In spite of these ultra-French fashions the girls were attractive and made a lot of friends. They saw a lot of the Thrale girls (daughters of Mrs Piozzi by her first husband) and of Charles Kemble who, though the girls' uncle was actually a month or two younger than Sally. Then there were Charles Moore, a younger brother of the hero of Corunna, and Thomas Lawrence, now in his mid twenties, and his sister, and a great friend of theirs, Sally Bird. Lawrence was now an A.R.A. and had recently, in spite of his youth, succeeded Sir Joshua Reynolds as Principal Painter to the King. The young people had evening parties in each other's houses, they went to exhibitions and picture galleries together and, of course, to the theatre. They had picnics in the country that was still so close to London, and they went to places like Ranelagh, where they could dine and dance and afterwards walk in the gardens listening to music.

During the summer the girls went to stay with their Aunt Fanny Twiss (now getting very stout) and her children at Catton in Norfolk, and then they joined William and Sarah who took Nuneham Rectory again. Sarah went on with her modelling, she was doing a head of George, and the others had the usual pleasant summer holiday. They had one excitement. 'George, dear little soul,' wrote Sarah, 'has escaped being dangerously hurt, if not kill'd . . . by almost a miracle. The accident . . . happened from their being forced to jump out of the little Market Cart which Mr Siddons had ordered to indulge the children in a drive.' Mr Siddons and Maria were involved in the accident too. They are both cripples at present,' Sarah added, 'each with a wounded leg, but I hope they are in a fair way to get better.'

In October Sarah felt she must get back to work, but she went, not to London, but to Ireland. In spite of all his promises Sheridan was still not paying properly and she said she would not go back to his company. The Irish tour was a success, but she still felt far from well. She was going through a time when everything seemed too much for her; she was expecting another baby and she worried about Sally's and Maria's health. They were delicate girls; Sally suffered from horrible attacks of asthma and they both caught colds easily which always went to their chests. 'They take no care of themselves and I have so much to *do* and to *think* of, that they *should* do,' Sarah complained to Mrs Piozzi . . . 'I don't know why, but I could weep at every word I write to you.'

Part of her worries came from Drury Lane again. After the Irish tour she relented once more and went back to Sheridan and to his new theatre, to open on 21 April. She thought it marvellous, but was worried about its size.

'Our new Theatre is the most beautiful that imagination can paint,' she wrote to Mrs Whalley. 'We open it with *Macbeth* on Easter Monday. I am told that the banquet is a thing to go and see of itself. The scenes and dresses are all new, and as superb and characteristic as it is possible to make them. You cannot conceive what I feel at the prospect of playing there. I dare say I shall be so nervous as scarcely to be able to make myself heard in the first scene.'

Sarah was justified in her fears – the new theatre was so enormous it was hard to be heard in it. The proscenium arch was 43 feet wide and 38 feet high and there were four tiers of boxes rising to the magnificent ceiling. The décor was impressive and as lavish as it could be and Sheridan had also introduced methods of moving scenery in a way never before considered possible; all sorts of effects were possible on the stage now. John Kemble even had a real lake for one play. The iron safety curtain, too, was considered a marvellous innovation.

There were many drawbacks, however, to the new theatre because of its size. All the actors were harder to hear and had to slow down both speech and action. This made everyone inclined to be ponderous and much of the spontaneity went out of the acting.

After *Macbeth*, which was a tremendous success, Sarah did not play again until after her seventh and last child, Cecilia was born, on July 25th of that year. 'Such a lumping baby,' Sarah said she was, but added, 'I bless God that I have brought you as perfect and healthful a Baby as ever the sun shone on.' She was delighted to have Cecilia, but all the summer she still felt depressed and nervy. 'My whole family,' she wrote, 'are gone to Margate, whither I am going also; and nothing would make it tolerable to me, but that my husband and daughters are delighted with the prospect before them. I wish they would go and enjoy themselves there, and leave me the comfort and pleasure of remaining in my own convenient house, and taking care of my baby.'

By the end of the summer, however, Sarah really was better and more cheerful, and felt she could cope with Sheridan and Drury Lane. Sheridan was still being unsatisfactory. Even though the enormous theatre was full nearly every night, players were still not getting all their salaries. He paid something, of course, but never in full and no one had their arrears. He could only get away with behaviour like this because there were so few theatres in London. If he had had more competition he would have had to pay.

Because she was not getting her full salary Sarah had to go off on tour again in the summers of 1796 and 1797. Great star that she was, she had to take exhausting touring work in order to make enough money to live in the style to which they had become used. And they still were exhausting tours. 'Here I am,' she wrote, 'sitting close in a little dark room, in a little wretched inn, in a little poky village called Newport Pagnell. I am on my way to Manchester, where I am to act for a fortnight; from whence I am to be whirled to Liverpool, there to do the same. From thence I skim away to York and Leeds; and then, when Drury Lane opens – who can tell? For it depends upon Mr Sheridan, who is uncertainty personified. *I have got no money from him yet*; and all my last benefit, a very great one, was swept into his treasury; nor have I seen a shilling of it. Mr Siddons has made an appointment to meet him today at Hammersley's. As I came away very early, I don't know the result of the conference; but unless things are settled to Mr Siddons's satisfaction, he is determined to put the affair into his lawyer's hands.'

It was lucky that Sarah felt better because tiresome things continued to happen. John gave up the management of Drury Lane – he said he could not work with Sheridan any more – and far worse, made a fool of himself by trying to make love to a young actress in her dressing-room against her will and had to write an apology through the papers. The gossip about this Sarah found hard to bear, and then to crown all there was another attack on her in the Press saying she was mad! It is not surprising with so many things to distract her that she did not see that Thomas Lawrence had fallen in love with Sally.

Sally was not a girl to be swept off her feet at once and at first she did not believe Lawrence meant what he said, but as time went on and he seemed completely absorbed in her she began to believe him. He was an exceptionally good-looking man and when he wished to be, fascinating, and Sally fell deeply in love with him. The engagement, if it was an engagement, was not official and neither Sally nor Lawrence said anything to her parents.

Before very long Sarah began to suspect what was happening, but she thought Sally young enough to wait a bit and as she did not want to start things moving she said nothing to William. And then, Sally began to realize that though Lawrence still came to the house ostensibly to see her, he was paying much more attention to Maria who, at eighteen and a half was extraordinarily beautiful.

Whatever Sally suffered when she realized this she kept to herself.

She did not even blame Maria or Lawrence – she thought Maria much more attractive than herself and she did not believe that her sister had tried to steal Lawrence away from her. Maria had always thought Lawrence attractive, and when she realized that it was she and not Sally he was coming to see, she fell head over heels in love with him at once.

Sally was so reserved and quiet and showed so little feeling that Maria truly did not feel guilty. She thought Lawrence and Sally had had a passing fancy for each other that had just worn off, but for all that she did find it a little embarrassing to see Lawrence at home in front of Sally, and she kept on arranging to meet him either in the park or in his studio in Greek Street. She and Lawrence told Sally Bird of their love and Miss Bird rather enjoyed her role of confidant and assistant and was helpful in arranging these meetings, and taking the notes Maria was always writing and bringing back Lawrence's answers.

Maria's best time for meeting Lawrence was in the evening when Sarah was at the theatre and she managed to see him often. Sally must have known something of what was going on, but because she could neither bear to seem jealous nor to speak about it, she said nothing. Maria was far too much in love to think about her health and never imagined that running out of warm rooms into cold streets insufficiently wrapped up would do her any harm, but the colds she kept catching and the feverish hurry and emotion she was in made her feel quite ill. Her agitation got much worse when Lawrence formally asked to be allowed to be engaged to her and her parents would not give their consent. William thought the engagement quite out of the question. He could not see how Lawrence could support a wife when he was still supporting most of his brothers and sisters. Sarah was almost as much against it as he was, though for a different reason. She was anxious about letting Maria marry a man who, she suspected, had already treated another of her darling girls rather badly.

Lawrence, usually spoiled and fêted, was not used to rebuffs and immediately became distracted. Maria was simply more than ever determined to marry him.

Secret meetings, however, became far more difficult now that her family knew of their feelings for one another, and Maria had to be both cunning and deceitful and even to tell lies in order to meet him. One day she pretended to have gone to the theatre to see *The Castle Spectre* when really she had been with Lawrence. She wrote

to Sally Bird, 'I came home so late that I went to my room directly
and would not ring for Candles that they might fancy I had been
in a great *while*. I *felt* how to dress myself absolutely, and came down
about the middle of dinner and my Father ask'd me where I had
been! I told a *story* and there was an end of it. Sally is getting better
I hope; she has been very ill and is still weak.' (Poor Sally was feeling
so forlorn and wretched that she had had a bad attack of asthma.)
'. . . I gave exactly the same account of the play last night as you
did, but you did not seem enough shock'd and pleas'd with the Ghost
of Evelina . . .'

Of course this sort of thing could not go unnoticed for long;
Maria's health would not stand it for one thing and she became ill.
Then, because she could not see Lawrence, she became frantic and
Sarah and William were alarmed. They saw with dismay that it was
her unhappiness that was making her ill and she was so delicate that
it really looked as if she might go into a decline. After a great deal
of discussion they agreed that they must withdraw their objection
and the engagement was allowed.

The moment her parents relented Maria got better, though the
doctor continued to be gloomy about her health. He knew that she
had tuberculosis and feared that she would never get well, but her
family did not realize this and were full of hope that she was on the
way to recovery. Sally continued to behave like an angel; she made
no scenes, nursed Maria devotedly and said nothing to anyone about
her feelings. At the end of January she wrote to Miss Bird saying
that Maria had been allowed down to the drawing-room and was
'recovering her strength and good looks every day . . .' She added,
'Here she must remain, Dr Pierson says, during the cold weather,
which means, I suppose, all the winter . . . But surely if every confinement was supportable,' poor Sally goes on, 'it must be to Maria,
for . . . the visits of her *first friend* are unremitted and should (should
they not?) console her for everything.'

Dr Pierson's treatment of a patient with tubercular lungs would
certainly not be followed nowadays and was not approved by everyone then. Mrs Piozzi wrote scornfully, 'Shutting a young, half con-
sumptive girl up in *one unchanged air* for three or four months would
make any of them ill, and ill-humoured too, I should think. But *it's
the new way* to make them breathe their own infected breath over
and over again now in defiance of old books, old experience and
good old common sense.'

Perhaps if she had been happy, in spite of such treatment, Maria would have got better, but as the days went on she saw, with growing unhappiness, that Lawrence was turning back to Sally. Maria was naturally selfish and capricious and illness made her fretful and irritable and every time Lawrence came to see her he saw Sally too, and saw her sweetness and unselfishness. He heard her sing (she sang delightfully and composed quite a number of her own songs, which were charming) and as he compared the two girls he began to feel very strongly that he had made a terrible mistake.

Maria might be sick, but she was no fool and at once she began to see what was happening. One day, when Sarah and Sally had gone to Covent Garden to see a new play, she wrote to Sally Bird, 'I agree with you that nothing can be so delightful as the *unremitting* attention of those we love, but where shall we find constancy enough in this wicked world to make us happy!'

Maria and Lawrence became engaged in the first week in January, but the 5th of March the engagement was at an end, broken off by Lawrence. Sally, who had still said nothing of her feelings, hoped that Maria was not too broken-hearted. It did not look like it, she thought. She wrote to Sally Bird, 'It is now near a fortnight since the breaking off and Maria is in good spirits, talks and thinks of dress and company, and beauty as usual. Is this not fortunate? Had she *lov'd him* I think this event would almost have broken her heart. I rejoice that she did not.'

But Maria, though she put a brave face on it, was unhappy, and even more angry and bitter. She wrote to Sally Bird in a very disillusioned and bitter way and talked of wishing to die. Of course being ill did not help her, giving her as it did so much time to brood.

Most men would have let some weeks at least go by before speaking to Sally, but Lawrence, in love, never considered anyone but himself, and when he and Sally went to Miss Lindwood's Exhibition of historical and other scenes done in needlework, he told her how his feelings had changed a second time. Sally refused to listen to him; she could hardly believe him and she could not bear to think of how much it would hurt Maria. Lawrence rushed straight back to Great Marlborough Street to tell Sarah and created a frightful scene. Sarah called it a 'terrible visit' and said she had to go down on her knees to prevent his rushing in to Maria to blurt out the truth to her. She believed it would kill Maria if he did. Lawrence behaved like a madman, raving about the two girls and his adoration of Sally and threatening suicide until he almost cowed even Sarah. She felt strongly the best thing for both her daughters would be to forget him -- a man so selfish and unfeeling, who seemed quite blind to what he was doing to Maria, would make a deplorable husband. But this, of course, he would not hear of, and by his threats of violence to himself, by his heartrending distress and just by sheer emotion, he finally forced her to give him some sort of promise that in the distant future perhaps he might be allowed to approach Sally again.

Lawrence then stormed away leaving poor Sarah to pull herself together as best she could so that she could face Maria as if nothing had happened.

16 Sally and Maria

It was a wretched time for everyone. If they had not all loved each other so much it might have been more difficult, but not more painful, because they would not then have been so sympathetic to each other. William was not so unhappy, he was just furious with Lawrence for jilting Maria, which was all he knew. Sarah had not dared to tell him that Lawrence now wanted to marry Sally, because if this had even been suggested his anger would be doubled. Sarah was torn between pity for Maria and anxiety about Sally. She could hardly believe any girl would want to marry a man so unstable and fickle, but one could never be sure. Certainly not when the man was as attractive as Lawrence.

Maria was very miserable, though she made great efforts to hide what she was feeling. She was suffering not only the agonies of being thrown over by the man she loved, but was also frantic with jealousy; she knew, though they never spoke of it, the reason for Lawrence's change of heart. She was not angry with Sally, but she could not bear to think Lawrence might be happy after all, and with her sister.

Naturally Sally was not as miserable as the others. To know that Lawrence loved her after all was very heart-warming, but she was pulled in half between her head and her heart. Although she was still in love with him she did think Lawrence had behaved badly and she hated to think of Maria being hurt. She had to suppress all her feelings about Lawrence for Maria's sake, and listen to her bitter railing against him in silence.

For Maria was intensely bitter. So much so that both Sally and Sarah believed it was only her pride that had been hurt – a painful emotion, but easier to bear than a broken heart. She seemed out-

wardly cheerful enough for Sally to be able to write about her as
she had to Miss Bird. The two sisters took what was a very similar
experience as differently as possible. When Sally believed she was
forsaken she honestly wished nothing but good to both Lawrence and
Maria, but Maria's reaction was that it was desperately unfair that
she should have to bear unhappiness and that Lawrence was unworthy of all the sacrifices she had made for him. Lawrence, of
course, had asked her for no sacrifices, nor had she made any except
those of speaking and behaving truthfully, but from the moment the
engagement was broken off her bitterness towards him grew and
grew.

Things were not made easier for her by being ill and confined to
the house. To cheer her up Sarah invited people in as often as
possible for the evening. Maria appeared to enjoy these parties, but
her health did not improve much – in her state of mind it was not
likely that it would.

Though Maria was the more unhappy of the two, Sally's position
was very difficult. She could not hint to Maria that she was in love
with Lawrence or he with her, and she had to hide the fact that they
were writing to each other. Lawrence was even begging to be allowed
to come and see her. It shows how blind he was to other people's
feelings that he could ever have considered doing this. Sally sent
him a brisk reply to this suggestion.

'You cannot be in earnest,' she wrote, 'when you talk of being soon
again in Great Marlborough Street . . . Neither you, nor Maria, nor
I could bear it. Do you think that, tho' she does not love you, she
would feel no unpleasant sensations to see attentions paid to another
which once were hers? Could you bear to pay them, could I endure
receiving them? Nobody need know what passes; from me they
certainly will not. I will try to make myself easy since my conduct is
no secret to her whose approbation is as dear to me as my life (her
mother); but I shall have much to endure . . .'

Sarah really did not know what to do about the girls, nor how
to get them out of the emotional tangles they were in. She knew that
Sally and Lawrence were writing to each other, but she was still
completely against any idea of marriage between them, not only
for Maria's sake, but because she did not believe anyone could be
happy with a man like Lawrence. She would have liked to send him
right away, but she did not think it wise to coerce Sally and she
was frightened of what Lawrence might do if he were thwarted
too much. He was so violent and unpredictable that there was no

knowing what scenes he might not make if he were cut off from Sally completely. And scenes of any kind could only hurt Maria still more. At the back of her mind was the fear that he might commit suicide.

To her relief, as the weeks went on and the warmer weather came Maria's health improved and she seemed to be getting over the shock. By the middle of April she wrote a much more cheerful letter to Sally Bird, with nothing in it about dying or wishing for death, but looking forward to getting well. She was hoping, as Sally had said nothing, that they had both finished with Lawrence. 'I am almost recovered now,' she wrote, 'and if nothing throws me back I hope I shall soon be able to go out; it appears to me that I should be very like myself if I could take a walk, and feel the wind blow on me again.' In a postscript to this letter she does sound quite like her old self. 'Charles, *our Uncle* is here, and desires I would give you his *love*, not his compliments, *oh, very well!*'

During the whole of this family crisis Sarah was rehearsing and then playing the very emotional part of Mrs Haller in *The Stranger*. This was a new kind of play and everyone was talking and arguing about it. In the same letter to Sally Bird Maria said, 'You have heard, I dare say, of this new Tragedy of *The Stranger*, it is the most affecting thing, I'm told that was ever seen, even men *sob* aloud. I wish very much to see it, is it not strange that one should like to cry? as if there was not enough of it in reality. Sally went, and she never was so affected before she says . . .'

The Stranger is a play about a woman who runs away from her husband and children with another man, then becomes deeply sorry for what she had done, and is finally forgiven by her husband and taken back to him and their children. This seemed absolutely immoral to many people then – to forgive a woman who behaved like that was undermining family life. Arguments about it raged, and of course, as everyone wanted to see it in order to see how dreadful it was, the theatre was packed and the play was performed again and again.

As Sally saw Maria's health and spirits improve she began to wonder if after all she and Lawrence could be happy together. On 23 April she met him by chance and the next day she wrote to him, 'I will tell you more on Thursday. Yes, I will *tell* you; for if it is fine I mean to walk before breakfast . . . I shall be in Poland Street before nine. You have the key of Soho Square; shall we walk there? Oh time, time, fly quickly till Thursday morning! . . .' This was the first time they had met by appointment. Sally goes on: 'Have you

taken your ring to Cowen's . . . have they told you it is a TRUE
LOVER'S KNOT? I bought it for you, I have worn it, kissed it,
and waited anxiously for an opportunity to give it you. Last night,
beyond my hopes, it presented itself. You have it, keep it, love it, nor
ever part with it till *you return my letters!*' The remarks about her
letters refer to a pact they had made that if Lawrence ever stopped
loving her – the inference being of course that he never would – he
was to return her letters. Sally goes on, 'I never should have sung as
I do had I never seen you; I never should have composed *at all*.
Have I not told you that the first song I ever set to music was that
complaint of Thomson's to a Nightingale? . . . You then liv'd in my
heart, in my head, in every idea . . . *You did not love me then*, But
NOW! oh, mortification, grief, agony are all forgot ! ! !'

Although Maria was (they hoped) getting over Lawrence, William
and Sarah were anxious to move her out of London; her health
would probably be better in the country and there was no chance of
her meeting Lawrence. She had expressed a longing for Clifton, so
Sarah wrote to her old Bath friend, Penelope Western, who was now
Mrs Pennington and who lived in Clifton for advice about lodgings.

No one knows what happened between Lawrence and Sally between her letter and the time the family left London, but something
did. That letter was one of a girl deeply in love, but by the time she
got to Clifton she was beginning to wonder if she could ever be
happy with him. Perhaps she had seen enough of him to realize that
he thought only of himself. He seems also to have been jealous (and
if he was he would certainly have made frightful scenes) because
Sally wrote to Miss Bird begging her not to believe that she was
falling in love with Charles Moore. Like her mother Sally hated
scenes and these may have opened her eyes to what life with
Lawrence would be like.

The Siddonses left London and arrived in Clifton in June. They
had decided to stay a month there before Sarah went on tour again,
and for that month they took lodgings in 'a very beautiful situation',
looking over the river to woods opposite. Maria stood the journey
well and they all hoped that the 'fine and famous air' would soon
'restore her entirely to herself . .'

During this month Maria did not get much better, but she did
not get worse, and when the tour began Sarah was anxious to take
Sally with her. She thought it good for the girls to be apart for a
time and she was sure Maria would be happy with Mrs Pennington,
with whom she was to stay while they were away. Cecilia, though

only four, was sent to school because 'her prattling hurt Maria's head', and George was at boarding-school anyway.

Sarah found it hard to leave Maria, and she kept writing to Mrs Pennington for detailed news of the invalid. 'Dear soul, add still to the numbers of your favours by telling me every particular about her,' she wrote on 26 July. 'I know she went to the Ball, I hope it did her no harm. This weather has prevented her riding too; tell me everything about her pulse, her perspirations, her cough, everything.'

Though worried, Sarah had not given up all hope of Maria's recovery. If she was fit enough to go to balls, even if she did not dance, and to go riding when the weather was fine, it did look as if she were improving. Maria herself thought she was better. She and Mrs Pennington got on well, but at first she had not intended to tell her about her love affair. Then, by a pure coincidence, Mrs Pennington read aloud to her a book in which the hero fell in love with two sisters. This was too much for Maria, who broke down and blurted out the whole story of her love and disappointment. She also confessed her fear that after all Sally would marry Lawrence. She said she knew that he would never now want to marry her, even if she got well, but she dreaded the thought of Sally being his wife.

Maria had reason to think Lawrence fickle and unstable, and no doubt really believed he was a dangerous husband for anyone, but Mrs Pennington was sure that her hatred of Sally and Lawrence marrying came from jealousy and a vindictive determination that he, at any rate, should not be happy. Mrs Pennington thought he would make a disastrous husband for any girl, but she tried to make Maria see that Sally must be left free to make her own choice, without any interference from anyone.

Although she spoke like this to Maria, Mrs Pennington wrote at once to Sarah, begging her to use her 'parental authority' to stop Sally getting engaged to Lawrence. She did not think Maria had got over it and it would be too cruel for her while she lived.

As it happened Sarah had been nursing Sally who had had an attack of asthma, and of course they had talked of Lawrence. To Sarah's joy Sally had said, leaving Maria out of the matter altogether, she had made up her mind that she could not marry him. She was still in love with him in a way, but she had come to believe that they could never be happy together.

Sarah felt she was absolutely right and she told Mrs Pennington that she need not worry, but she also told her firmly that even if Sally had not been so wise she would not have used her 'parental

Above: The interior of the old Covent Garden Theatre and, *below,* the new auditorium which afforded 'the Publick improved accommodation and security'

These family portraits are from a lithograph by R. J. Lane made from some of Lawrence's sketches. *Left:* Cecilia Siddons (above), Sally Siddons (below); *right* George Siddons (above); Charles Kemble (below)

authority'. She would not coerce her daughters. 'In this *most* IMPORTANT *object of their lives*,' she wrote, 'it has always been my system that they must decide for themselves.'

Sarah had also had to nurse William, who had a bad leg, and with this and all her anxiety about both daughters, it was trying having to tour round the country from theatre to theatre, playing five nights here and three there, particularly as the company she was with was very bad. 'I am playing every night to full houses,' she wrote, 'but how the people can sit to see such representations is quite wonderful, for anything so bad I never yet beheld, and I have seen strange things.'

In August she went to Brighton and there played before the Prince of Wales and Lady Jersey, whose relationship she thoroughly disapproved of. She did not want to meet Lady Jersey, but was too famous to escape this. 'This place is crowded with people I know nothing of,' she wrote to Mrs Pennington. 'So much the better for I am ill dispos'd to gaiety. I have played twice to fine Houses, and the Prince frequents the Theatre with great attention and decorum. He has issued his sublime commands (which, it seems, nothing but death or deadly sickness will excuse one from obeying) to have me asked to supper with him, which I, disliking the whole thing, had declin'd; but when I came to talk it over with Mr Sid. he thought it best that I should recant my refusal : and so I went to sup at Mr Concannon's, where, as I had feared, I met Lady Jersey. . . . Lady Jersey is really wonderful in her appearance. Her hair was about an inch long all over her head, and she had ty'd round her head one single row of white beads; this I thought ill-judged. She certainly wou'd look handsome if she wou'd not affect at forty-eight to be eighteen.'

To add to the trouble of the family at the moment, William's leg got worse. 'William is quite lame, absolutely walking on crutches,' Sarah wrote. 'Something is the matter with his knee, but whether Rheumatism or Gout, or what it is, Heaven knows'; It was so bad that he was terribly afraid of becoming permanently crippled, which made him depressed and rather cross.

Sarah and William had been buoying themselves up with the hope that Maria was getting better, but when they got back to Birmingham from Brighton they had a letter from Mrs Pennington which made them realize there was no hope that she would ever get well. Maria was suddenly so much worse that they decided they could not leave Mrs Pennington alone to cope, and as William was too crippled and Sarah could not get away, Sally must go to Clifton at once. Mr Macready, the manager of the theatre, offered to go with her. Sarah hated parting with her, but a few hours later she was thankful Sally had gone, because Lawrence arrived unexpectedly in Birmingham, ostensibly to see his sister, really to see Sally.

Sally had no idea that he would come, but she had told her mother to tell him, if the opportunity arose, that she had definitely decided that she could never marry him. Lawrence came round at once to see Sarah and, in fear and trembling, she gave him Sally's message. He refused to accept that this decision was final and Sarah had a dreadful time with him. The next thing she heard was that he had gone posting off to Clifton after Sally, whom he was determined to see for himself. Sarah wrote to Mrs Pennington in a panic to warn her of this. No one knew what he would do. She believed he was nearly frantic, half with remorse about Maria lest his treatment of her had made her worse, and distractedly in love with Sally.

17 Sally's Promise

Maria was so delighted to see Sally that for a little she seemed to rally, but both Sally and Mrs Pennington knew that this improvement would not last if she realized that Lawrence was still wanting Sally to marry him. They had a difficult time pretending to Maria that nothing was happening and at the same moment dealing with Lawrence, because as soon as he arrived in Clifton he sat down and wrote pages to Mrs Pennington about his adoration of Sally, saying he could not live unless she became his wife, and begging Mrs Pennington's help. By this time he had made himself believe that Maria's love for him had just been the 'weakness of a sick fancy' for which he was not in the least to blame. He had apparently forgotten that he had asked her to marry him and that they had been formally engaged. He felt no remorse about her – Sarah was quite wrong when she believed he did – he was just afraid that this 'sick fancy' might be a bar to his marriage with Sally, and for that reason he agreed that it was much better that Maria should not know he was in Clifton or that he was still hoping to marry her sister.

Mrs Pennington and Sally believed that Maria was beginning to suspect that something was brewing because she became very exacting, wanting one or other of them with her all the time, which made it difficult for them to discuss Lawrence's letter as fully as they wanted to. They finally agreed that the best thing would be for Mrs Pennington to go and meet him.

The interview took place in a field behind the Boar Inn, where they walked up and down. Lawrence was as wild as Mrs Pennington had feared, but though she disapproved of such frantic goings on she could not help feeling sorry for him because he seemed so unhappy. It was a very hot, sunny day and the heat and agitation at last made her 'flump down upon a dusty bank' – she could not go walking up and down with him any more. Although she was so tired, and sorry for him, she kept her head and refused to be over-impressed by his ravings and threats of suicide. She was almost sure he was putting on an act to terrify her and she told him firmly that she had seen scenes better acted before on the stage, and if he wished to secure her friendship, or hoped for her good offices, a rational and composed behaviour was a better way of obtaining them.

Lawrence realized that he was doing himself no good and calmed down, especially as she agreed that he should see Sally if she had no objection. She also promised to let him know every day how the girls were. In spite of the fact that Lawrence refused to admit that he was in any way to blame for Maria's illness, he was as anxious for her recovery as anyone because he had an uneasy feeling that if Maria died Sally would think him partly responsible for her death and refuse to forgive him.

Sally did meet him. No one knows what happened, but from a letter she wrote to Sarah after it she had obviously promised him nothing. Lawrence began to think seriously he must have a rival; he could not believe that otherwise any girl could withstand him. He was far too egotistical to make any effort to understand Sally and he never grasped that if he had been less self-centred and more controlled he would have had a much better chance with her. As it was, all his wild ravings only made her realize more clearly than ever how very little chance she had of being happy with him.

Sally refused to meet him more than once, so Lawrence left Clifton and went back to Birmingham where he had another shattering scene with Sarah. It lasted for three hours. He paced about 'in agonies' and so upset her that two or three times she was on the verge of fainting and was quite unable to act that night after he had gone. After enduring it Sarah could well imagine what Mrs Pennington had been through too and wrote to her, 'I shudder to think on the effect this wretched madman's frenzy has had on you. I know the effects too well, for he well knows how he has terrified me into my toleration of his love for Sally by the horrible desperation of his conduct.'

How she managed to calm him at the end of their interview she does not say, but she did and he went away 'composed, grateful for my forgiveness . . . and detrmin'd steadily to pursue a course of conduct which shou'd regain his credit'. She had not much faith in such promises because she felt that there was 'little to be expected in points of improvement from a man who at the age of THIRTY appears to have so little control over himself.'

To her relief, after leaving Birmingham Lawrence did not bother Sarah personally. He pestered Mrs Pennington with mad letters, sometimes full of sorrow for poor Maria's bad health (the extraordinary man even did a crayon portrait of Maria at this time – unfortunately lost – and even had the nerve to send it to her) but mostly full of unbalanced ravings about Sally. Mrs Pennington wrote answers to them and did her best for him, but it was impossible to do much because she could not advise Sally to accept him.

Maria became perfectly aware that there was something going on between Sally and Lawrence again and was very unhappy. She got steadily worse and about a month later William and Sarah got the dread summons to hurry to Clifton.

Both girls were thankful to have their mother with them. Sally was just getting over a bad attack of asthma and Maria could hardly bear Sarah out of her sight. Sarah was a tower of strength to everyone, even managing to keep cheerful though Maria's looks were heartbreaking – she was so thin she looked like a skeleton covered with skin.

The Siddonses had taken rooms just opposite the Penningtons and about ten days after they got to Clifton they decided to move Maria from Mrs Pennington's house to theirs. Angelic as their old friend had been and helpful as she was still ready to be, they had imposed on her long enough. Maria stood the move very well – she still had surprising energy on occasions though everyone knew her death must be very near. They did not know if Maria realized this too; they thought not, but on the evening of Friday, 5 October, she asked to be told the truth. Sally and Mrs Pennington were alone with her because Sarah had been persuaded to go and lie down when Maria asked her old friend if she could ever be well. She had been very restless during the early part of the night, wanting the doctor called and saying she was sure she was worse, but eventually Mrs Pennington calmed her and she lay quiet. Then suddenly, perfectly calmly, she asked if she were dying.

Although they had all kept on pretending to her that she would get better, Mrs Pennington believed that she ought to be told the truth now, and after a glance at Sally, who nodded, she did so. Maria did not seem surprised at the news, nor much distressed. She said she was 'more composed and comfortable than she had been through her illness' and when she spoke again it was about her belief in God and her sorrow for the things she had done wrong.

But though she thought she was prepared for death, she was still obsessed by thoughts of Lawrence and Sally. Jealousy, determination that Lawrence should not be happy, or fear for Sally's happiness were a jumble of motives that even Maria could not have disentangled. No one knows which predominated – we only know what happened from a letter Mrs Pennington wrote to Lawrence. Maria called Sally over to her and told her that she had only one fear for her future 'Promise me, my Sally,' she said, 'Never to be the wife of Mr Lawrence. I *cannot* BEAR to *think* of *your* being so.'

Though she was heart-wrung about Maria, Sally tried to avoid giving any promise; however much she had made up her own mind not to marry Lawrence she did not want to give Maria, or anyone else, a positive promise about it. 'Dear Maria,' she said, 'think of nothing that agitates you at this time.' But Maria was not to be put off. She insisted that far from agitating her it was only this promise that would quiet her mind. In great distress Sally said, 'Oh, it is impossible!' She meant it was impossible to promise, but Maria thought she meant it was impossible that she and Lawrence could ever marry. With a sigh of thankfulness she sank back and, to the relief of the others, appeared to put the whole matter out of her head. When Sarah came in, which she did early on Saturday morning, Maria seemed only concerned with her approaching death and wanting her mother to read some prayers for her.

But Lawrence was not out of her mind, and later that day she said to Sarah that Sally had promised she would never marry him. Poor Sally was too honest even to acquiesce silently in a lie. The emotion of the moment was too much for her and in her distress and pity for Maria she said, 'I did not promise, dear, dying Angel, but I WILL and Do, if you require it.'

Maria fixed her great dark eyes on her. Then she said, 'Thank you, Sally; my dear Mother, Mrs Pennington, *bear witness*. Sally, give me your hand.' Almost as if mesmerized Sally did so and Maria went on, with terrible emphasis, 'You promise never to be his wife. Mother, Mrs Pennington, lay your hands on hers.' Reluctantly, slowly, almost as if they too were hypnotized by the determination of the dying girl, they did so. 'You understand? Bear witness,' she said. Unable to speak Sarah and Mrs Pennington signified they acquiesced. Maria then looked at Sally again. 'Sally, sacred, sacred be this promise.' Her energy was so fierce, and her eyes so bright that they were awestruck and no one could speak. Maria pulled her hand from under theirs and pointing its thin, emaciated forefinger at Sally added slowly, *Remember me*, and God bless you!'

Although all three knew in their hearts that Maria had no right to extract such a promise from Sally simply because she was dying, they could not say anything. Maria was fading before their eyes and any remonstrance seemed cruel. She had seemed too, more like a creature from another world than a jealous girl. That at least was what Mrs Pennington felt and what she wrote to Lawrence.

The change in Maria was so marked after this that Mrs Pennington realized properly just how unhappy she had been over Sally and Lawrence. She now became completely at rest. She even got some colour in her face and looked almost pretty again. She was not only ready to die, but perfectly happy and unafraid. She said good-bye to everyone in the house humbly, simply and with deep affection. At two o'clock on the Sunday morning, 7 October, she died. She was nineteen years old.

18 The End of the Romance

Directly after Maria's funeral the Siddonses left for Bath to stay with the Whalleys. Besides their grief, Sarah and Sally were in great anxiety about Lawrence and what he would do, and on top of everything Sally became ill. As always happened to her when she was upset, she had a bad attack of asthma. They both knew that Mrs Pennington had written at once to Lawrence telling him, not only of Maria's death, but of the promise she had made Sally give her.

Used as they were to outbursts, Lawrence's reply shocked them all. From its appearance it might have been written by a madman with what was obviously a shaking hand, and with underlining nearly a quarter of an inch thick. Its wording gave the impression of a man nearly beside himself, and there was not one glimmer of sympathy for any of them in the whole note. It was dated five days after Maria's death and ran :

'It is only my Hand that shakes, not my mind.
I have play'd deeply for her, and you think she will still escape me. I'll tell you a Secret. *It is possible she may. Mark the end.*
You have all play'd your parts admirably ! ! !
If the scene you have so accurately describ'd is mentioned by you to *one Human Being*, I will pursue your name with execration.'

Mrs Pennington felt bitterly hurt. She was worn out with nursing and the strain she had been under for weeks (much of it due to Lawrence) and she thought it horrible of him to write her such a letter. She had really tried to be sympathetic and kind, and had taken a lot of trouble for him. She replied almost at once. 'I thank you,' she wrote in bitter irony, 'You have made a *Grateful* return for a long and painful task, imposed on me by YOURSELF, which I have endured patiently, and discharged with integrity and the truest, tenderest sympathy.' She went on to say that she thought he was unworthy of any further help, that she ignored his threats, and that she did not want ever to hear from him again.

The Whalleys were as sympathetic and kind as usual and the Siddonses were glad to have such friends to go to, but by 13 October they had to return to London because Sarah was due to act again. She told Sheridan that she could not be in anything that reminded her of all she had been through, and finally they agreed on *Measure for Measure*. Little as she wanted to start work again she did in fact find it a help to have the theatre to go to. It took her mind off her grief and worries.

The moment they got back to London Sally, who had not really recovered, had another attack of asthma. Sarah was thankful that Patty Wilkinson could come to stay with them. She was the daughter of the Tate Wilkinson whose snuff Sarah had so much enjoyed, and was about Sally's age. Sarah had asked her before Maria's death, but she had not been able to come then. Now she was more than welcome. They were all fond of her and she became like one of the family. When she first arrived she was only coming on a visit, but somehow she stayed on and on – because they wanted her to – and it became a settled thing that she should live with them. She was devoted to Sarah, who very soon came to look on her as another daughter.

As soon as Mrs Pennington got Lawrence's 'diabolical letter', as she called it, she sent it on to Sarah. She regarded it as the letter of a man so mad that she advised Sarah to tell not only William, but John Kemble too about the whole affair, in order that Sally might be protected. She honestly believed that Lawrence might do something outrageous. 'While he has ONLY the *timidity* of WOMEN to operate on, and to oppose him there is no saying *what* he may not *attempt*,' she wrote.

Sarah showed Sally Lawrence's letter and she reacted to it as the others had done. 'I seriously believe,' she wrote to Mrs Pennington, 'that he is, at times, quite mad; there is no other possibility of accounting for his conduct. Poor wretched creature! Let him inflict still farther torments on those who love and are interested for him, *he will still be the most tormented.*'

In spite of all Sally's protestations Sarah was anxious about her. She might meet Lawrence by chance any day, and who knew what would happen then? He had calmed down a little and had even written to Mrs Pennington, trying to get her to forgive him and to open a correspondence again (which she refused to do), but she believed he was so emotional and uncontrolled that it was almost certain he would make a scene the moment he saw Sally. She heard he was haunting the Twisses, and that Fanny was, in a way, encouraging him. It was not that Fanny thought Sally would be happy with such an impetuous creature, even if her wretched health allowed her to marry at all, but she thought Maria had had no right to extort such a promise and that Sally ought to take no notice of it. Promises extracted in that way went for nothing, in her view.

Sally agreed with her about this. As she recovered from her first grief at Maria's death she could think more dispassionately about the whole episode and Sarah knew that she had come to the conclusion that Maria was 'actuated as much by resentment for *him* as care and tenderness for *her* in it'. Lawrence, as might be expected, refused to consider for a moment that such a promise was binding. For a little time after Maria's death he did not dare to get in touch with Sally personally, but he had not given up hope by any means. With his usual complete misunderstanding of other people he tried to approach her through Patty Wilkinson, who very naturally refused to have anything to do with him. After being rebuffed by Patty, Lawrence took to hanging round Great Marlborough Street. On one occasion Sally saw him from the window, looking earnestly towards the house. She turned away from the window, although she knew he saw her. She half expected him to come to the door, but he did not.

Up to now Sarah had still said nothing to William, but shortly after this she had to tell him. The Siddonses went to church one Sunday and Lawrence was there, obviously in the hope of seeing Sally. Neither she nor Sarah would look at him, and this upset him so much that he rushed away to the Twisses and made one of his terrific scenes. 'He terrified Mrs Twiss so completely that both she and Mr Twiss have told him that they shall either of them quit the room at the very first mention of the subject,' Sarah reported to Mrs Pennington, after Fanny had poured out to her what a terrible time they had had. Sarah realized that now she must tell William, and did so. She wrote, rather sadly, to tell their old friend how he had taken it. 'With that coldness and reserve which had kept him so long ignorant of it . . . no it is not his *fault*, it is his *nature*.'

William had grown rather unsympathetic and withdrawn from his family. He was very fond of them all, but he was getting irritable (his painful leg may have had something to do with this) and he had got out of the way of joining in things with them. He did not even see any point in saying anything to Sally now about Lawrence, until Sarah insisted that he must, and told him Sally would think him most extraordinarily unkind if he did not. Some of William's lack of sympathy may partly have been because he had not been told anything about it before, but it was partly, too, because he could not understand how Sally and Sarah had ever had anything to do with Lawrence. In his view no decent man could behave as Lawrence had done and he thought his family were quite unnecessarily concerned with such a hopeless, unreliable, uncontrolled person.

Lawrence might be all these things, but Sarah was still not sure that his fatal fascination might not weaken Sally if she began to see him again, particularly as Sally had admitted she did not believe she would ever again love anyone as she had loved him. Sarah was unnecessarily anxious. Sally was no fool. She had come to realize, poor girl, that the Lawrence she loved existed only in her imagination. She wrote to Mrs Pennington, 'The creature *I would have lived and died* for, EXISTS NO MORE, or, as I have before said, *never did exist*. Time and circumstances have discover'd to me a character which nothing could tempt me to unite myself to.'

She grew more and more sure about this, and in December wrote to him in reply to a letter of his saying so decisively that she would not marry him, that even he seems to have accepted it as a final dismissal.

19 Last Years of Greatness

The brightest thing in the Siddons household that winter was Cecilia, now five and a half. She was an enchanting little girl, lovely to look at and according to Mrs Piozzi the 'most extraordinary of all living babies. Many I have seen, but none of such premature intellect. It is a wonderful infant seriously.' The theatre was so important to all the Siddonses that, though she was so young, they began to take her there. For friendships' sake, but reluctantly because it was such a bad play, Sarah had agreed to act in Mr Whalley's *The Castle of Montval,* and as a treat, Sally took Cecilia to see it. On her own Sally would have been bored, but Cecilia was so thrilled by everything that she kept all the rest of the party amused. A few days later they took her to see *Bluebeard,* the story of which she knew. She kept everyone near her entertained by her comments and 'she has done nothing but act Sister Anne upon the tower, waving her handkerchief ever since', wrote Sally.

Sally was not well all through the winter, with frequent attacks of asthma. Although she did not change her mind about marrying Lawrence she was not yet indifferent to him and she was made unhappy by rumours of his chasing this young woman or that. They all went to Bath in January, for Sarah to complete her engagement there that she had had to put off at the time of Maria's death, but Sally was too ill to see her mother play.

Sarah had other problems besides those of her family. Sheridan still owed her an enormous amount of money and William again said she should not act in the new play, *Pizzaro* until she was paid. Sheridan badly wanted Sarah in it (though he was doubtful if she would like her part which was that of a common camp follower) but he did not want to ask her to come back, nor did he want to pay up. All through the season they bickered back and forth, until William changed his mind again. He began to be afraid that if she gave up acting for Sheridan she never would get her money, so disgusted as he was with the whole arrangement, he advised her to take a part in this new play.

Pizzaro was a translation from the German and Sheridan had great hopes of it. He made it a lavish production, but he was such an irresponsible person now that the principal actors did not get the last act until the day of the performance. It is even said not until after the play started! Sheridan is said to have been in the prompter's room, drinking port and sending down the dialogue as fast as he translated it. It was typical of him to be so dilatory and extraordinary as he so much wanted the play to be a success, but of course he knew that John, who was also in the cast, and Sarah always responded magnificently to any great challenge. They did so on this occasion with what can only have been a brilliant improvisation.

Sheridan and Sarah argued all the way through rehearsals about her part, Elvira. He wanted to make her a common, sluttish woman, but Sarah insisted that the author, Kotzebue, had intended Elvira to be much more noble than that. John refused to take any part in the controversy, but he knew who he thought would win, and he was right. 'My sister,' he said, 'made a heroine out of a soldier's troll.'

Sheridan was a bundle of nerves on the opening night, but after seeing Sarah's performance he admitted that she was right. She came on looking like an amazon, in a plumed helmet and was wonderful. *Pizzaro* ran for over thirty performances and made Sheridan a lot of money, but his players got very little of it – he was up to his old tricks again.

Because of his dishonesty Sarah had to set off on her usual provincial tour again that summer. She was still unhappy about Sally who, she told Mrs Pennington, 'had had a sad winter of it', and whose health went on being very poor. She became so ill in August that for some days they thought she would die. Sally thought so too, and having seen Maria die of consumption she not only dreaded it, but was convinced she had it. She began to get better as soon as the doctor made her believe that she neither had tuberculosis, nor need ever have it.

As the new Drury Lane season drew near William had his usual dither as to whether to let Sarah play for Sheridan again. He had paid her some of her arrears, but by no means all and neither

William nor Sarah knew what was the best thing to do. In the end they decided she should not go back. Sheridan once again tried to believe that he could do perfectly well without her, and once more made the discovery that he could not – if he wanted to fill his huge theatre he had to have Sarah. He promised once more that all William's terms should be met, that he would pay Sarah all he owed her and that her current salary should be paid regularly without fail, so they gave in once more. He also persuaded John to take over the management of the theatre again.

Sarah's popularity was as great as ever, but she was getting older and was tired enough to be thankful to have an excuse to take a rest and not go on tour during the summer. Her excuse was William's health, he was far too unwell to be left alone. The whole family went to Broadstairs, and afterwards to Brighton, where they were joined by Mr and Mrs Kemble, now nearly in their eighties.

Sally got stronger during the summer. She had seen Lawrence occasionally and when they got back to London in the autumn she did so again, but they merely acknowledged each other. Sarah, on the other hand, often saw him at the theatre. She had decided to let bygones be bygones and she always had a soft spot in her heart for the brilliant creature she had first met as an infant prodigy in Devizes. She never mentioned at home that she saw Lawrence, but Sally knew it perfectly well. She wrote to Miss Bird, 'I believe he scarcely ever misses a night when my Mother performs when he generally pays her a visit in her dressing-room. This I hear not from my Mother, for unless I force her to it, she never mentions him, but if she would give me an opportunity I would tell her something which I know would greatly please her, which is that I am now *at last myself perfectly convinc'd* that he is become *entirely indifferent towards me.*'

There was one minor flare up between them which shows that if they had gone on seeing each other Sally might well have married him in the end. They met in the theatre by chance one evening and he cut her dead. Sally was hurt and Sally Bird was drawn in once more as a go-between. Lawrence accused Sally of some slight or neglect – how he dared one cannot imagine – which she denied indignantly. Sarah, who dreaded the whole affair starting again, was furious with Sally Bird and they had several stormy scenes about it, but in the end the danger died away and Sarah forgave her.

This really was the end of Lawrence's and Sally's love affair except for the effect it had on Sally's health. She continued very delicate, with frequent terrible attacks of asthma. William's rheumatism, too, was getting worse and in the summer of 1801 he went to Bath to try the cure there. To crown everything Sarah herself had a bad attack of erysipelas round her mouth, which caused the most terrible irritation and burning. She had already had one attack, but this was worse. It cleared up after about a month, but the whole year was a trying one especially as William lost £3,000 of the £10,000 Sarah had made. Without saying a word to her he had invested this money in Sadler's Wells theatre, and lost it all.

In spite of all that Sarah had been through she still looked wonderful and that autumn, when she appeared in a magnificent dress of black velvet and sables (she had come to prefer black or white to colour) she looked, so the papers and public said, as beautiful as she had ever looked in her life. For a woman of forty-six this was quite a triumph.

One other nice thing happened this year, Henry made a successful first appearance on the London stage. Sarah was not lyrical about him, but she was pleased. She wrote to Mrs Fitzhugh (who had recently become one of her most devoted admirers and friends) 'My son Henry's success has been a very great comfort to me. I do think, if I can divest myself of partiality, that it is a very respectable first attempt.'

Beautiful as she looked in black velvet and sables, she did not look young any more. She was beginning to lose her slenderness and though she was still shapely she was definitely putting on weight. She had played most of Shakespeare's heroines, young or middle aged, but so far she had never tried Hermione, in *The Winter's Tale*. She acted it for the first time in the spring of 1802.

It was very nearly her last part. She was standing as the supposed statue, her draperies floating round her, when a scene shifter in the wings noticed a smell of burning. Her muslin dress had floated over the lamps that were lighting her from behind the pedestal on which she was standing, and caught fire. The man crawled forward on his face and put it out. If he had been even a few seconds later her whole dress would have gone up in flames and she would probably have been burnt to death. 'I have well rewarded the good man,' she wrote, and she did not only show her gratitude with money – she found out that his son had deserted from the army, been caught and was due to be flogged. 'I have written myself almost blind for the last three days,' she wrote, 'worrying everybody to get a poor young man, who otherwise bears a most excellent character, saved from the disgrace and hideous torture of the lash, to which he has exposed himself. I hope to God I shall succeed. He is the son of the man – by me ever to be blest, who preserved me from being burned to death in *The Winter's Tale.*'

It was at the end of this season that she and William finally decided that they were finished with Sheridan and this time they kept to it. He was becoming increasingly dissolute, drunken and unreliable and John took the same decision. He went abroad with his wife for a long, much-needed holiday. He planned to take over Covent Garden Theatre when he came back and he was lucky enough to get Mrs Inchbald to carry on the negotiations for him while he was away. He was childless and quite wealthy and could afford a rest. Sarah, particularly after William's unfortunate speculations, could not. She went to Ireland for a long tour.

Only Patty went with her. William was too infirm and immobile for travelling and Cecilia was too young, so Sally had to stay at home to look after them. Sarah felt unusually depressed at going for so many months. She wrote a dreary letter to Mrs Piozzi full of foreboding and saying how miserable she was at saying good-bye to her family. She was sure she would never see her father alive again.

In spite of this anticipation of misfortune, Sarah cheered up once she had started. She and Patty stopped at Stratford-upon-Avon and Conway and enjoyed themselves in both places. Letters from England were cheerful too. Sally was having a good time and seemed perfectly happy. She wrote from Bath, on 2 June, 'We had several very pleasant parties before I left London. Charles Moore's pic-nic was quite delightful, it was such fine weather, the Temple Gardens so gay and the whole scene so beautiful. Bertie Greatheed dined with us and we walked with him to the Temple, where we arrived at half-past seven. We had tea and coffee; Dorothy Place and I presided . . . After tea we walked in the garden till nine, at which time a bell rings, after which no promenading in the garden is permitted . . . we had a pretty cold supper, and did not part till past twelve o'clock . . . On Wednesday we went to a party at Sadler's Wells, where we were very pleasant; and on Saturday Charles Moore sent us orders to see the 'Surrender of Calais,' and 'Fortune's Frolic'. How delightfully I laughed at 'Fortune's Frolic'.

One thing Sarah had to miss by being in Ireland was Henry's wedding. He married Harriet Murry, whom they all liked, though she was not a good actress. Sally's account of the day said, 'Miss Murray looked very beautiful, in a white chip hat, with a lace cap under it, her long dark pelisse tied together with purple bows, ready for travelling. Henry was so nervous that Miss Payne was nursing him up with good things. At nine, my father, Mr Murry &. &. and I went to church.' It was a very emotional wedding. The ceremony 'had hardly begun before poor Henry turned as pale as death, and shook from head to foot so that he was obliged to hold by the rails near him to support himself.' The bride was in nearly as bad a state; she cried so much she could hardly speak. All this weeping and shaking was only nerves because Henry and Harriet were devotedly fond of each other. The emotion was catching because almost every-body cried. Henry was in a complete dither all through the service. He cried out 'I will' before it was necessary, and 'he wanted to put on the ring, too, before the proper time'. But in spite of all this they got married properly and went off to Birmingham. William gave Harriet a 'handsome coral necklace, bracelet and earrings', but Sally was furious that her wedding present to the bride, a ring, did not arrive in time.

The Irish tour was the usual success and so rewarding financially that Sarah originally intended to have a nice restful winter at home. George, through the Prince of Wales' influence, had been offered a cadetship in the East India Company and William thought they had had so many expenses in getting his outfit and in the renovations they were doing to Great Marlborough Street, that she had better go on working, and she decided reluctantly that he was right.

It was a pity Sarah did stay in Ireland because it meant she got to know the Galindos. Mrs Galindo was an actress, not a good one, and he was a fencing master. Sarah took fencing lessons from him because she was considering playing Hamlet again, an unwise idea which was sensibly dropped, and she saw a great deal of them both. She went for rides in their curricle and promised to help Mrs Galindo get a job when she returned to London and Covent Garden. They made a tremendous fuss of her, being thrilled at having so great a celebrity for a friend. Sarah enjoyed this to begin with; later she deeply regretted becoming so friendly with them.

She had been right in her premonition that she would not see her father again. He died on 6 December. Although she had been expecting it, it was a shock and it made her very sad; she had always been so fond of him. She hated saying good-bye to George, too. He came over to Ireland and spent a fortnight with her before he sailed for India. She could hardly bear to part with him, but he had such good prospects in his job that she tried to be as cheerful as she could.

I

During all this Sarah had no reason to be anxious about Sally's health. On 2 February she had a letter from her describing herself as well and gay, and George had not said anything about her health being bad. She had no idea therefore that Sally was ill, and made arrangements to play in Cork. William, from some misguided idea of not bothering her said nothing until on 10 March he wrote to Patty and told her Sally was ill. Even then he advised her not to let Sarah know. Naturally Patty disregarded this and showed Sarah the letter. Although William had not made too much of it, Sarah was alarmed and wanted to set off for England at once, but to her dismay the weather was so bad with the equinoctial gales that no ships were sailing. She felt desperate, though she was reassured by another letter from William, dated two days later, saying that Sally was better and that there was no need for Sarah to come home, she could go on to Cork as arranged. Unwillingly, with a foreboding and heavy heart, she went.

Then to her astonishment she got no more letters and as the days went on with no further news, her anxiety got unbearable. She wrote to Mrs Fitzhugh, who was nobly helping to nurse Sally, 'Oh, why did not Mr Siddons tell me when she was first taken so ill? I should then have got clear of this engagement, and what a world of wretchedness and anxiety would have been spared to me! . . . Has she wished for me? But I know – I feel she has . . . Would to God I were at her bedside . . . Will you believe I must play tonight, and can you imagine any wretchedness like it in this terrible state of my mind?'

She played at Cork for a week, then she could bear it no more and told the manager of the theatre that she must go home. It was a great blow to him, but he understood what she was feeling and released her from her contract and she and Patty hurried at once to Dublin, as they thought it might be easier to get to England from there than from Cork.

Both William and Mrs Fitzhugh had written regularly, but the letters had been delayed by the bad weather, and then sent to Cork, as they did not know of her change of plans. When she found no letters at Dublin she was much too upset to think rationally why they were not there and wrote a distraught complaint home, unjustly accusing William and Mrs Fitzhugh of heartlessness.

The gales were still bad, but as the boats were sailing Sarah and Patty crossed at once. The moment they got to Holyhead they posted straight on to Shrewsbury, and there were met by a letter from William. It was written on the 24th of March, and warned Sarah to expect the gravest news, but begging her to 'remember the preciousness of her own life and not to endanger it by over rapid travelling'. William knew, as he wrote it though he did not say so, that all the speed in the world would not bring her back in time to see Sally alive – she was not expected to last the night.

While Sarah was reading his letter Patty was called from the room. When she returned Sarah knew from her pale, awestruck face what she had to say. Sally was dead.

20 Final Curtain

It was a long time before Sarah got over the shock and grief of
Sally's death. For a day she stayed at Shrewsbury, lying cold and
motionless on her bed. Her brothers rallied at once to help her;
John wrote directly he heard and Charles hurried to meet her and
take her home, as William was too infirm to do this.

She was too prostrated to face further work at once, and she spent
the summer at Birch Farm, near Cheltenham, where she rested and
took the waters. Patty and Cecilia were with her and the peace of
the place, 'reading under the haystack', 'musing in the orchard' and
'rising at six and going to bed at ten' helped her to face and overcome her sorrow. She was so devoted to Sally and it was so terrible
to her that she had not been with her at the end.

Towards the end of September she returned to the stage, this time
to Covent Garden. With Mrs Inchbald's help John had got part
ownership of the theatre and all the stage management, and of
course he wanted Sarah to play for him. He was not at all pleased
when the Galindos arrived in London, Mrs Galindo claiming that
Sarah had promised to get her work. John could not bear this couple
who, according to him, were 'persons it was a disgrace to know', and
he thoroughly disapproved of Sarah's friendship with them. She
defended them for some time, as long as she could, in fact, even
though her feeling for them cooled, until she too realized how impossible and ungrateful they were. They borrowed £1,000 from her
which they never attempted to repay, and much worse than this Mrs
Galindo finally rewarded her kindness to them by publishing a
pamphlet called *Mrs Galindo's letters to Mrs Siddons; being a cir-
cumstantial detail of Mrs Siddons' life for the last seven years; with*

several of her letters. In it Sarah was accused of wrecking the Galindos' home, alienating with 'satanic barbarity' Mr Galindo's affections from his wife and of ruining their lives. Sarah had certainly been unwise ever to become friendly with such people, but that was her only fault. As for saying that she tried to make Mr Galindo fall in love with her, it was absolute nonsense. The pamphlet fell flat, but even though no one who knew her, or even those who read it, believed the accusations, it caused Sarah a lot of annoyance. Her friends rallied round her immediately, but no one likes having such things published about them, even if they are not true. Nearly everyone agreed that to take any action at law against Mrs Galindo would only give the whole wretched business more publicity, and besides which, as she wrote to her nephew, Horace Twiss, who did want her to prosecute, 'What would be the result of such a persecution? Damages or Imprisonment, I suppose, and failure of the first, what should I gain by inflicting the second? There are three children, all under nine years old too, that must be reduced in either case to a state of wretchedness and perhaps absolute want of bread ...'

In the 1804–5 season Sarah played sixty times, nearly as often as in her youth. She loved working for John instead of Sheridan. She was as popular and admired as ever, but she was getting older, and the following season she had a bad attack of rheumatism and could not play much. She had electrical treatment for this and said it felt like sparks of burning lead being poured into her veins. She screamed so much during the treatment that William expected people to break into the house to see if anyone was being murdered. A treatment so painful was certainly drastic, but agony or not it did her good.

William's rheumatism was not, unfortunately, getting any better – he was getting worse every day. Bath seemed the only place where he got any relief and he went back there. This decided them to give up the Great Marlborough Street house; which was too big for them now anyway, and move into lodgings. Sarah, Cecilia and Patty moved into rooms in Princes Street, Hanover Square, kept by Mr and Mrs Nixon.

It was not only Sarah's health that kept her off the stage during the 1805–6 season. All the theatre-going world had gone mad about a so-called infant prodigy who, for a time, drove all older players into the background. Henry William West Betty was a boy of eleven who had been taken to see Sarah act. He immediately became completely stage-struck and badgered his parents until they let him go on the stage. In the most extraordinary way the moment he was seen he became all the rage. He did not play children's parts, but many of the great adult ones, including some of Sarah's own, and Richard III and Hamlet. He was a precocious child and a brilliant imitator, but if he had not been so young no one would have thought anything of his performance. As it was people went mad about him, even the critics. Sarah was less easily taken in and summed him up very accurately. Someone said to her one day that he believed the boy would 'eclipse everything that had been called acting in England'. Sarah looked at him for a minute, then she said, 'He is a very clever pretty boy, but nothing more.' She was perfectly right, of course, that was just what he was. By the next season he was hardly noticed and then he faded out of the public mind.

The Siddonses did not really like lodgings and in the April of this year Sarah did something she had always wanted to do, took a house in what was then country, at Westbourne, near Paddington. It had a large garden and she built herself a studio where she could do her modelling. William was delighted with the house – he even wrote one of his poems about it, and longed to live there, but his rheumatism became so bad again that he had to go back to Bath.

Sarah was fifty-one when she bought Westbourne Cottage and she was definitely getting stout. She was still shapely and was tall enough to carry off her added weight, and her complexion and face were as beautiful as ever. She still filled Covent Garden whenever she acted, which she did thirty-four times that season. She was earning the highest salary paid to anyone, £50 a night, a prodigious figure at that time.

It was at the end of this season that old Mrs Kemble died, and early in the next year Sarah had an even deeper loss. William became so ill in Bath that she cancelled her engagements and went down to him. He seemed to get much better and when she was asked to act in Edinburgh early in 1808 she thought it was safe to leave him, but she bitterly regretted doing this, because he was suddenly taken ill and died on 11 March. Though she rushed back from Edinburgh she was too late to be with him at the end. A little later she wrote to Mrs Piozzi . . . 'There is something so awful in this sudden dissolution of so long a connection, that I shall feel it longer than I shall speak of it. May I die the death of my honest, worthy husband; and may those to whom I am dear remember me when I am gone, as I remember him, forgiving and forgetting all my errors, and recollecting only my quietness of spirit and singleness of heart . . My head is so dull with this stunning surprise that I cannot see what I write . . .'

Mrs Piozzi always maintained that Sarah and William did not get on and did not care for each other, but from this letter it does not appear so. William did get rather difficult; he was sometimes selfish, usually pompous and, latterly, frequently irritable, especially when his leg was bad. But it is never easy to be the mediocre husband of a brilliantly successful wife and Sarah realized this perfectly. Although she was the breadwinner and the success she never tried to take from him what she considered his proper place as head of the family and she loved him as an affectionate, responsible and honourable man. William sometimes found her trying too, but he never stopped loving and admiring her.

As she began to get over William's death Sarah looked forward to another harmonious season at Covent Garden with John, but in September, just after the season opened, all the hard work John had put into the theatre went up, literally, in smoke. On the 20th Covent Garden burned to the ground. Luckily it happened when the theatre was empty, at 4 a.m. Sarah did not leave it till midnight and all seemed as usual then, though in fact the fatal bit of wadding was smouldering away behind some scenery. Patty Wilkinson said that she had smelt a strong smell of burning while she sat in John's box, and that she had spoken of it to several of the stage-hands and dressers as she went to Sarah's dressing-room, but they had assured her it was only the smell of the lamps she noticed. The play was *Pizzaro* and the wadding had been shot out of a gun and no one had noticed where it fell, or that it was alight.

It was the most terrible loss to John. He lost not the theatre alone, but all his irreplaceable manuscripts and first editions of plays, some unpublished musical scores by Handel and Dr Arne, Handel's magnificent organ, as well as all the costumes and scenery he had spent so much on. Sarah lost a tremendous lot too . . . 'All the precious and curious dresses and lace and jewels which *I* have been collecting for these thirty years – not one, no, not one article has escap'd,' she told someone in a letter. 'The most grievous of these *my* losses is a piece of Lace which had been a Toilette of the poor Queen of France (Marie Antoinette); it was upwards of four yards long and more than a yard wide. It never could have been bought for a thousand pounds, but that's the least regret. It was *so* interesting . . .'

The shock and the dismay were frightful, but the Kembles showed the stuff they were made of, and John took his loss 'with, Sarah said, 'a manly fortitude, Serenity, and even hope . . .' He had solid grounds for hope because he had so many offers of help that he was able to start rebuilding at once, and he had great plans of making Covent Garden even more wonderful than the new Drury Lane. Strangely enough five months later Drury Lane also burnt to the ground. It was the finish of poor Sheridan, and bankrupted him completely.

Covent Garden was finished in time to open on 18 September the following year. *Macbeth* was the play. It had cost so much to build (it was larger than the old theatre and very handsomely decorated) that John found he had to raise the seat prices. A section of the regular theatre-goers determined to resist this. They got together and someone organized them very well. They arrived on the first night and allowed each player to receive his first applause on entering, after that anything he or she had to speak was howled down with insults and cries of 'Off! Off!' Then they began what came to be known as the O P (Old Price) dance. The audience beat with their feet and sticks and shouted rhythmically, 'O P! O P! O P!' Some people held up placards on which were indecent or insulting remarks. Even when Sarah came on, after the first applause she too was howled down and could not make herself heard. The Kembles once more showed the stuff of which they were made. Neither she nor John faltered and because they did not the rest of the company followed their lead. They went on with the play (quite inaudible) as if the audience were not shouting, stamping and booing. 'Perhaps the finest dumb show ever witnessed,' said the *Covent Garden Journal* next day.

Although she appeared calm on the stage, Sarah was disgusted with such behaviour and refused to appear again while such scenes went on. John had to put up with organized rioting of this sort every night for three months; he tried to hold out but in the end, because it was ruining him, he had to give in, at least partially and reduce some of the seats to their old price.

When the riots were over and Sarah came back she was just as popular as ever, and she played for the rest of that season and through the next two, but at the end of the last she made the momentous decision to retire. It was a very hard decision to make because she appeared as popular as ever, but she was nearly fifty-seven and she felt she would be wise to go before her powers failed. She made her final appearance on 29 June 1812.

The play was *Macbeth* and the theatre was packed to danger point. At the end of the sleep-walking scene the applause became almost out of hand and the audience demanded that the play should end there – her last scene. As it was clear everyone wanted this, the management agreed. Then, after an interval the curtain rose on the climax of the evening. Sarah, dressed simply in white, was sitting at a table. As the applause thundered on and on she rose and came forward, and when at last it died down she began her farewell address, a poem written for her by Horace Twiss.

'Who has not felt how growing use endears
The fond remembrance of our former years?
Who has not sigh'd, when doom'd to leave at last
The hopes of youth, the habits of the past,
Ten thousand ties and interests, that impart
A second nature to the human heart,
And wreathing round it close, like tendrils, climb,
Blooming in age, and sanctified by time!

'Yes! at this moment crowd upon my mind
Scenes of bright days for ever left behind,
Bewildering visions of enraptur'd youth,
When hope and fancy wore the hues of truth,
And long forgotten years, that almost seem
The faded traces of a morning dream!
Sweet are these mournful thoughts: for they renew
The pleasing sense of all I owe to you,
For each inspiring smile, and soothing tear –
For those full honours of my long career,
That cheer'd my earliest hope and chas'd my latest fear.

'And though for me those tears shall flow no more,
And the warm sunshine of your smile is o'er:
Though the bright beams are fading fast away
That shone unclouded through my summer day:
Yet grateful memory shall reflect their light
O'er the dim shadows of the coming night,
And lead to later life a softer tone,
A moonlight tint – a lustre of her own.

'Judges and Friends! to whom the magic strain
Of Nature's feeling never spoke in vain,
Perhaps your hearts, when years have glided by,
And past emotions wake a fleeting sigh,
May think on her whose lips have pour'd so long
The charmed sorrows of your Shakespeare's song:
On her, who, parting to return no more,

> Is now the mourner she but seemed before :
> Herself subdu'd resigns the melting spell,
> And breathes, with swelling heart, her long,
> Her last Farewell.'

The last time of anything is usually sad, and the last play for a great actor or actress almost intolerably moving. Sarah was nearly overcome, many of the audience were in tears, and so was John when he came forward to lead her from the stage. The audience could hardly take in, and Sarah hardly bear to think, that they would never see her acting there again.

Without doubt her contemporaries thought she was the greatest actress there had ever been. James Ballantyne, a theatre critic wrote, 'We can only say that no sculptor or painter, in the sublimest flights of his fancy, ever embodied . . . a creature so formed, so gifted, to agitate, awe and astonish mankind by her professional powers, as her whose matchless form, face, voice and eye are now finally withdrawn from our publick admiration.' Washington Irving, who did not see her until she was fifty, said : 'I can hardly breathe while she is on the stage. She works up my feeling till I am like a mere child.'

When Sarah was older she almost certainly became too statuesque in movement for our taste and probably too impassioned in her acting, but when she was at the height of her powers it seems no audience could have resisted her. It was not only that she had such an unusually beautiful face and figure, or that her acting was so intelligent, natural and sensitive, but she clearly had that magic power of moving people, which can never be learnt, is the supreme gift of an actor, and is timeless. In some parts she must have been unique. It is possible there never will be a greater Lady Macbeth however long the theatre lasts and the plays of Shakespeare are staged on it.

If we were sitting in the theatre today and the curtain could rise on that dark-eyed, lovely creature, transformed into the character she was playing, we should agree, I believe, with the audiences who did see her that there never was, and never will be, a greater tragic actress than Sarah Siddons.

Postscript

Sarah was not unhappy in her retirement though she missed the theatre greatly. Her worst time was in the evening. 'This is the time I used to think of going to the theatre,' she said. 'First came the pleasure of dressing for my part; and then, the pleasure of acting in it; but that is all over now.'

She did give readings after she retired, dressed in white and sitting in front of a red screen. Though she remained stout she never became shapeless and her face and skin were extraordinarily young looking. She read beautifully and gripped her audiences as much as ever. She did act once or twice more too, always for a benefit, but she remained on the whole in retirement.

She had several more sorrows. She lost Henry in 1815 – he died of consumption as Maria had – and in 1823 her beloved brother John. Fanny, Mrs Piozzi, Mr Whalley and Lawrence all died before she did. Cecilia and Patty remained with her – they were as devoted as ever. Her eyesight became bad, but she always looked younger than her years and was able to get about a good deal. She often went to the theatre, and she saw Charles's daughter, another Fanny, make her début on the stage.

It was in April 1831, when she was just seventy-six, that she had her last, fatal attack of erysipelas. She got it on an ankle, and though it was bad, it seemed to yield to treatment and she told her doctor 'she had health to sell!' Thinking herself better than she was, she went for a drive and caught a chill. She became very ill; the erysipelas attacked her other leg and she had frightful suffering. Then the doctors saw with dismay that gangrene had set in and there was no hope. At the very end the pain left her and she seemed to sleep. On the morning of 8 June, at eight o'clock, Cecilia, watching by her bed with her mother's hand in hers, saw her noble features settle into a beautiful, unmoving serenity. Sarah Siddons was dead.

Bibliography

Boarden, James, *Memoirs of J. P. Kemble*, 1825
Boarden, James, *Memoirs of Mrs Siddons*, 1827
Boswell, James, *Life of Dr Johnson*, 1887
Campbell, Thomas, *Life of John Philip Kemble*, 1832
Campbell, Thomas, *Life of Mrs Siddons*, 1834
Congreve, William, *Complete Works*
Davies, Thomas, *Memoirs of the Life of David Garrick*, 1780
Fitzgerald, Percy, *The Kembles*, 1871
Fitzgerald, Percy, *Life of David Garrick*, 1868 (1899)
Ffrench, Yvonne, *Mrs Siddons*, 1936
Kennard, A., *Mrs Siddons*, 1893
Kemble, Frances Anne, *Record of a Girlhood*, 1878
Knapp, O. G., *An Artist's Love Story*, 1904
Marinacci, Barbara, *Leading Ladies*, 1962
Nicoll, Allardyce, *Eighteenth Century Drama*, 2 Vols. 1925–7
Nicoll, Allardyce, *The Development of the Theatre*, 1927 (1948)
Nicoll, Allardyce, *British Drama*, 1925
Nicoll, Allardyce, *The English Theatre*, 1936
Otway, Thomas, Plays of
Parson, Mrs Clement, *The Incomparable Siddons*, 1909
Pope, W. MacQueen, *Theatre Royal, Drury Lane*, 1945
Rowe, *The Tragedy of Jane Shore*,
Royde-Smith, Naomi, *The Private Life of Mrs Siddons*, 1932
Southern, Richard, *The Georgian Playhouse*, 1948
Southern, Richard, *The Oxford Companion to the Theatre*, 1957
Thrale, Mrs, *Thralania*, Ed. by Katharine Balderstone, 1951
Tosenfeld, Sybil, *Strolling Players and Drama in the Provinces, 1660–1765*, 1939

I have quoted two letters of Sally Siddons' which were published in the *Nineteenth Century* of April 1905. They were sent to that journal by Lady Priestly. The Editor allowed Mrs Parson to quote from them in *The Incomparable Siddons*.

Index

Regent, The, 92
Reynolds, Sir Joshua, 66, 76, 85, 101
Richard III, 12, 42
Rivals, The, 51
Romeo and Juliet, 96
Romney, 66
Runaway, The, 41

Sedgerly Park School, 14, 22
Seward, Anna, 50
Scott, Walter, 51
Sheridan and Company, 45
Sheridan, Richard Brinsley, 45, 51, 52, 60, 61, 70, 73, 74, 81, 84, 85, 87, 94, 97, 99, 100, 101, 102, 103, 125, 136
Sheridan, Thomas, 51, 52, 55, 56
Siddons, Cecilia, 99, 102, 112, 124, 133, 139
Siddons, Elizabeth Anne, 52, 54, 76, 93
Siddons, Frances, 50
Siddons, George, 90, 98, 100, 101, 112, 129
Siddons, Henry, 31, 53, 56, 57, 63, 76, 100, 217, 128, 129, 139
Siddons, Maria, 50, 53, 76, 98, 100, 101–20, 122
Siddons, Sally, 36, 53, 76, 98, 100, 101, 103, 104–23, 125, 126, 128–31
Siddons, Sarah, birth of, 7; first appearance on stage, 7; sent to school, 11; first public appearance, 12; agrees to marry Siddons, 16; goes to live with Greatheeds, 20; auditions for David Garrick, 22; rejoins her father's company, 24: marries William Siddons, 25; appears for the first time as Mrs Siddons, 26; leaves her father's company, 27; joins Chamberlain and Crump, 27; birth of son,

Henry, 31; leaves Chamberlain and Crump, 32; joins Mr Younger's Company, 32; joins Garrick's company, 35; birth of daughter, Sally, 36; first appearance at Drury Lane, 38; Drury Lane contract not renewed, 45; plays Lady Macbeth for the first time, 46, 47; joins company in Bath, 49; daughter Maria born, 50; daughter Frances born, 50; Thomas Sheridan sees Sarah in Bath, 51; birth of daughter Elizabeth Anne, 52; returns to Drury Lane, 55; appointed Preceptress in English Reading to the Princesses, 65; appears at Command performance, 69–70; first Irish tour, 67–72; birth of son George, 90; death of daughter Elizabeth, 93; leaves Drury Lane, 97; returns to work for Sheridan, 99; birth of daughter Cecilia, 102; death of Maria, 119; leaves Sheridan again, 128; death of Roger Kemble, 129; death of Sally, 131; goes to Covent Garden Theatre with John Kemble, 132; death of William Siddons, 134; final appearance, 136; death of, 139
Siddons, Mr, 9
Siddons, William, 9, 12, 15–19, 20, 22, 24, 25, 26, 27–29, 32–34, 35–37, 44, 48, 52, 53, 54, 57, 58, 60–62, 67, 76, 77, 80, 81, 83, 93, 97, 98–100, 101, 113, 117, 123, 126–9, 130, 131, 132, 133, 134
Steevens, Mr, 90
Stranger, The, 110
Suspicious Husband, The, 42

Tempest, The, 12, 31
Thornlea House School, 11